TEL

The human resource implications

Telework:
the Human Resource Implications

John and Celia Stanworth
Future of Work Research Group
Polytechnic of Central London

Institute of Personnel Management

First published in 1991

Phototypeset by The Comp-Room, Aylesbury
and printed in Great Britain by
Short Run Press, Exeter

British Library Cataloguing in Publication Data

Stanworth, John, 1942–
  Telework: the human resource implications.
  I. Title   II. Stanworth, Celia
  331.25

ISBN 085292 465 8

Contents

Contents   vii

Preface

Telework – working remotely for an employer using computer and telecommunications technology – has attracted a great deal of recent media coverage, because of its potential to change the shape of work organizations, as well as changing the lifestyle and working conditions of individual workers. Some commentators, for example, Alvin Toffler and the Henley Centre for Forecasting, have predicted that teleworking could soon involve millions of workers operating from home; others have predicted the demise of the office as we now know it. These predictions contrast with the relatively small number of pilot schemes currently being developed and tested by employers, and with the reality of crowded commuter trains and traffic jams caused by people still travelling from home to work! As with many futuristic scenarios, the truth probably lies somewhere in between the two extremes: there will probably be gradual changes over time in the locations where work takes place, but 'pressing the flesh' is unlikely to go out of fashion and city centres and office complexes will still be populated into the next century.

Teleworking has in fact been technically possible for many years now. In the USA it was suggested by Jack Nilles in California as a way to solve the then oil crisis as far back as 1973. However, it is only recently that more employers have begun to realize that teleworking could provide a work pattern which they could use (not just for computer programmers and analysts) to solve their own particular human resource problems.

Even in periods of economic downturn, employers have found it difficult to recruit people with scarce skills. Telework can be used to retain existing staff or to access alternative recruitment sources among people who, for various reasons, are prepared to work at home all, or part, of the time. This potential workforce certainly includes people with young families, elderly dependants or people with disabilities. These potential recruits may be located within a short distance of the office or they could be physically very remote. People with the required skills could be employed in a satellite office relatively close by, or in another region of the country where employment costs are lower and potential recruits more numerous.

Another reason for considering some form of telework is to stabilize or reduce high office overhead costs. The trigger for considering 'flexi-place' arrangements by organizations has in several cases been the need to rationalize office usage. For example where operations continually spill over into more and more sites, or where new office building is being considered to accommodate growing numbers of staff, or current accommodation is crowded, telework may appear on the agenda.

Another pressure on employers to consider telework may come from their existing employees. They may be asking for a more flexible regime in terms of time and place for various reasons: a career-break mechanism for women starting families, or as a respite from the expense, stress and time wasted in travelling to and from work. It can also be used by employees moving house to a distant location who would like to keep their existing job, or people who may be temporarily disabled but want to carry on working from home during their recovery.

However, telework is still considered to be very novel, and seems at first sight to involve much greater complexities than more conventional patterns of work. Managers are often anxious about how to supervise remote workers and there do not seem to be many role models to follow. These factors tend to act as disincentives to employers.

This book is intended to offer managers a practical and realistic framework which will allow them to assess the costs and benefits of telework, and how such arrangements might work in their own particular organization. It also advocates a 'best practice' approach to human resources: its emphasis is primarily on treating all types of employee as full members of the organization, however physically remote or 'atypical' they may be.

John and Celia Stanworth

Acknowledgements

The authors wish to thank all the people who helped in any way during the production of this book. In particular Efrosini Haughton who wordprocessed the manuscript so quickly and accurately; Jos Thompson for technical information on computer hardware and software, and the companies and individuals who so generously gave us their time.

1

Telework: what it is and how much there is

What is telework?

Telework is not a job, but is a method of organizing work which is built around the processing of information. The individual, or group of people carrying out the work is remote from the employer, client or contractor for whom it is being done. The work involves the use of various kinds of electronic equipment, and the product of that work is communicated remotely, often but not always, using tele-communications links. Post or courier services might be used as an alternative. Figure 1 illustrates this in diagram-matic form.

The combination of electronics and the telecommunica-tions network opens up opportunities to:

- change the 'shape' of an organization,
- increase the scope of work done away from the office,
- free work from time and locational constraints.

There are a number of human resource problems which teleworking can help to overcome. These include:

- pressures to reduce and rationalize office overheads.
- the need to access alternative local labour markets:
  - women with children,
  - carers,
  - disabled people.
- the need to access alternative labour markets further afield:
  - in areas of higher unemployment,
  - in areas of lower fixed costs.

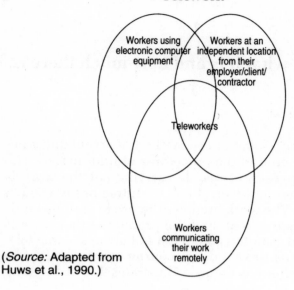

(*Source:* Adapted from Huws et al., 1990.)

Figure 1: *A definition of telework*

- the need for better quality and faster information feedback.
- the need to retain staff with scarce skills and experience by offering a more flexible work life.
- the need to keep staff 'on tap' at any time, including:
  - key senior executives,
  - financial analysts,
  - computer maintenance managers.
- the need to avoid disruption if a valuable member of staff is temporarily disabled or moves house to another location.
- the need to provide a career-bridge scheme for employees starting a family.

Employers' reasons for deciding to use telework have been extremely varied. During the recession of the early 1980s it was used as a way of coping with fluctuations in demand, cutting office overhead costs and managing redundancies. For example, the Rank Xerox networking scheme was designed to transform existing managers into self-employed owner-managers, with support along the way from the 'parent' company. In contrast, teleworking can be used in tight labour markets, and many of the schemes implemented recently lie within the 'Golden Triangle' of London, the South-East, the South West and East Anglia. This area has the highest overall percentage of both men and women in work in the UK and was the focus for much of the growth of service-sector employment in the late 1980s. These are difficult labour markets not only for professional and technical staff but in many places for more routine clerical and administrative staff. Coupled with this are high fixed costs and transport infrastructure problems. This is leading employers to look for alternative sources of labour, or make better use of their existing workforce.

How much telework is there?

There are no reliable figures of the extent of teleworking in the UK, or worldwide for that matter. No-one has attempted a nationwide survey large enough to estimate a 'global' UK figure. Most of the information on telework has come from a few case studies, and a lot of the literature focuses on the so-called 'Big Four': the Rank Xerox networker scheme; CPS/ICL; FI Group and the Department of Trade and Industry Remote Work Scheme (see Figure 2 for a selection of cases). Besides these there are many informal arrangements within firms of tele-homeworking schemes which have not been widely publicized. The job titles in Figure 2 demonstrate the growing diversity of jobs now being considered as suitable for telework. Another estimate of numbers comes from Catherine Hakim's Home-based Worker study for the Department of Employment, which estimated that in 1985 there were about 5000 home-based Worker study for the Department of Employment, which estimated that in 1985 there were about 5000 home-based teleworkers. Figures on home-computer ownership in a British Social Attitudes Survey in 1985 showed that one in 200 households had a computer linked to a main-frame through a modem, and it has been estimated by Brocklehurst (1989) that this represents between 10 000 and 15 000 households. We can assume that some of this hardware would be used by teleworkers.

Worldwide, telework appears to be most advanced in the United States, followed by the UK, France, Germany and Italy, according to the International Labour Office (ILO, 1990). In Scandinavia, Sweden has pioneered the development of rural telecottages, but in Norway, Finland and Denmark the development is more limited. There are also some schemes in the Netherlands and Switzerland.

There are a few examples of telework drawn from Australia and Canada, where it is considered by the ILO to be in its infancy. Japan is adopting satellite offices rather than home-based work in the Tokyo area. Offshore tele-work, particularly for American firms, takes place in Barbados, China, Eire, Jamaica, Mexico, Korea and Singapore. Australia uses subcontracted labour in Singapore and the Philippines.

world the range is generally fairly narrow. The teleworker workforce is predominantly made up of data-processing professionals, insurance representatives, word-processing staff, translators, or part of schemes for disabled people, according to Ursula Huws (1984).

In none of the countries of the world is telework very widespread, as yet. As Figure 2 shows, the numbers of people involved are often small. This is primarily because some of the schemes are currently at a 'pilot' stage. Most organizations plan to expand the teleworking workforce after a successful trial period.

Figure 2: *Case study examples from the UK*

Organization	Job Title	Location	Numbers
FI Group	Software programmers and managers	Home/ Local Centre	750 (varies) panel members
Rank Xerox	Professionals and management specialists	Homebased/ Clients/Local Centre	50–60
Chamberlain's	Personnel services consultants also programming and admin/secretarial	Homebased/ Clients/ Office Centre	119 + 150 associates
ICL Contract Programming Services	Systems designers, technical writers, publishers, trainers remote-work consultants	Homebased/ Clients/ office	250
Hampshire County Council	IT staff, social services staff, word-processors, inspectors	Homebased or Homebased/ Office	20 pilots
Project Frontline	Data processors, computer programmers	Local Centre	one centre now open
DTI Remote Work Project	Word processors, computer programmers, researcher, company secretary	Homebased (disabled)	58 (in 1990)
Allied Dunbar	Sales representatives	Mobile	3,500
Bull HN	Computer programmers	Homebased	8–10
DEC Ltd	Computer professionals	Homebased/ Office	3
	Computer maintenance staff	Homebased/ Office	?
Nottingham Building Society	Videotex editor, data processing staff	Homebased	11
Texaco UK	Sales representatives surveyors, negotiators	Mobile/ Homebased	400
Typing Plus	Word processors, proofreaders office services	Homebased	30
Fintech	Journalists	Homebased/ Mobile	6

Sources: Various

2

Ways of using telework

The combination of computers and modern communications links gives the employer a great deal of choice of work arrangements. In this chapter we will explore the different ways of using telework, with examples of existing schemes.

A variety of possible work arrangements

Figure 3 shows a network of possible combinations of work location and contractual arrangements. Position A represents the conventional office-based employee of a company: position B represents the other extreme, the archetypal 'electronic cottage' self-employed teleworker, much publicized by futurists and journalists. What the network demonstrates is that there are many different ways in which telework can be used, to match the strategies and objectives of different work organizations, and the types of jobs involved.

The main ways of using telework

The five main ways of using telework are:

1. Home/office combinations
2. satellite offices
3. local centres
4. home-based
5. mobile

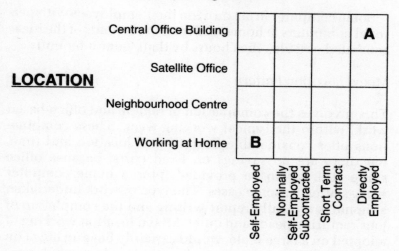

LOCATION

Central Office Building — A

Satellite Office

Neighbourhood Centre

Working at Home — B

Self-Employed / Nominally Self-Employed Subcontracted / Short Term Contract / Directly Employed

TYPE OF CONTRACT

(*Source:* Adapted from Brandt, 1983.)

Figure 3: *A variety of possible work arrangements*

Home/office combinations

Overflow pattern

This occurs where telework is used as an *addition* to the normal working week. Some financial analysts have computer set-ups at home to keep them constantly abreast of changing world markets. One well-known oil company keeps its senior executives in touch with the office when they are at home and even when they are at conferences abroad, by linking up the equipment wherever they are! This is often considered a 'perk' or badge of high office, but can of course mean that the executive is never really off duty.

Some computer firms provide their employees with personal computers at home, and reap the benefits of the ideas generated outside office hours by their 'computer buffs'.

Mixed Location Pattern

This involves the combination of remote and office-based work, *within* the typical working week. These combinations offer considerable flexibility of location and time, but there are no savings on fixed costs, because office space still has to be provided, plus a home computer work-station in some cases. The type of work undertaken at home is typically report writing and the completion of jobs requiring peace and quiet. Mixed location working, if adopted on a large scale, would certainly have an effect on patterns of commuting, and would reduce peak-time 'crushes', on the roads, railways and the Underground.

There is evidence of a considerable number of informal arrangements of this kind in Britain, among 'trusted', generally higher-status, employees. They are not widely publicized, but represent a growth of 'flexi-place' arrangements which offer advantages to both managers and managed.

Satellite offices

In the case of satellite offices, the technology can radically alter the overall 'shape' of the organization's structure, but for the employees working in such offices, the work pattern, supervision and control used is much the same as in a conventional office.

Ursula Huws (1984) has highlighted the problem of defining the difference between a teleworked satellite office and the computer-linked branch offices of, for example, a bank or building society. However, if a relatively small branch office is set up at a remote location, specifically to open up more favourable labour markets, rather than to serve local customers, we think it is reasonable to embrace this under the heading of telework.

Often, the satellite office is used to carry out 'back-office' functions, usually of a fairly narrow, stand-alone nature. Two London local authorities, for example, are planning to set up remote offices to deal with community charge payments, one in Sheffield, and another in Barnstaple, Devon. The Royal Borough of Windsor and Maidenhead set up a Remote IT Development Unit in Telford, Shropshire, as a response to recruitment and retention problems. British Telecom has also used this idea by processing directory enquiries for London in a Darlington exchange, and carrying out Freephone work in various locations around the country.

The reasons for setting up such offices are usually to gain access to a more plentiful labour supply, but also to cut office overhead costs. One successful example is a word-processing centre which was set up several years ago by Lloyds Bank in Newton Aycliffe in County Durham. This centre provides a service for 16 London branches. The information is dictated onto cassettes and sent to the centre, processed, and then sent back by computer link-up to the branches where it is printed out. The office costs have been cut by a factor of six, recruitment problems eased, and less paper generated.

A somewhat different concept is being developed by the Frontline Initiative. This is a co-operative venture between the National Economic Development Council (NEDC) and inner-city task forces, aimed at setting up a number of centres in older cities to train information technology workers, and provide work for them, mainly on contracts from firms based in the South-East of England. The first centre opened in Nottingham in 1990 and hopes eventually to employ around 150 people.

The most extreme form of the remote office idea is a set-up in another country or 'offshore'. America has the greatest number of these, located in several countries including Barbados, Mexico, and Eire. Typically, again, these are undertaking self-sufficient, back-office functions. For example, near Limerick in Eire, Neodata of Colorado have an office which receives batches of magazine subscription coupons nightly by air from America. These are entered into the computer database and sent by computer link back to America. Despite the transport costs, this is said to be cheaper than processing the information in the USA. The Eire government is keen to expand such schemes both to provide local work and also break the long tradition of emigration of young people from the country.

Local centres

There are several types of local, or neighbourhood, centres which bring computer and telecommunications facilities close to workers who are generally home-based, or away from the conventional office setting. These include commercial business service centres as well as 'dedicated' centres set up by a particular work organization for the exclusive use of their own workers.

Examples of commercial centres include British Telecom's 'Network Nine'. At the moment these operate in Central London, London Docklands, Aberdeen, Bracknell and one in Wales. A mix of commercial and altruistic services is provided by 'telecottages' or teleservice centres which are often associated with rural settings, but which could just as well be set up in inner-city or suburban areas. In small towns and villages, such centres are being set-up in redundant farm buildings (the Hope Valley in Derbyshire), local village halls, or unused classrooms within schools (Crickhowell School, for example).

One example of a 'telecottage' is Llangedwyn Mill in rural Wales, where an organization called the Tanat Cain Venture has been sent up. It provides training in computer skills and work for local people. The commercial work is often carried out for clients faraway in England, but a lot of the activity is concerned with strengthening the local community. There is a great deal of interest in developing more such centres, in order to revitalize rural labour markets and provide better quality jobs in country areas. There are only a few at present. The organization Action for Communities in Rural England (ACRE) now has a full-time worker, sponsored by British Telecom, whose job is to develop, encourage and publicize such ventures.

The other kind of local centre is set up by a work organization for the exclusive use of its own employees or subcontractors. Rank Xerox set up one such centre for its networkers in Stony Stratford. FI Group, who have about 750 project-based IT specialists working remotely, are now supplementing home-based work with neighbourhood work centres. These are open 24 hours a day, and provide secure access to clients' systems and support facilities. The centres are seen as supplementing, not replacing, work at home. They reduce isolation and communication barriers which can bedevil this kind of work. Obviously these centres are still quite rare and exclusive to remotely based organizations, of which there are still currently only a handful in the UK. They would not be feasible unless there were a reasonable number of remote workers in a local area. An alternative idea which has been suggested is a co-operative venture between various firms, to set up local centres in 'high street' settings, for the shared use of their remote staff.

Home-based

There are two types of home-based worker:

- those who work predominantly at home, but spend some working-time visiting clients and employers,
- those who work exclusively at home.

The first group includes IT professionals such as those

working for CPS/ICL and FI Group who spend part of their working time at clients' premises, and surveyors and property negotiators who work for Texaco and who spend part of their time visiting sites. The Training Agency has around forty Training Standards Inspectors covering the whole of Great Britain, who spend around one-third of their time at home and the rest carrying out inspections, or liaising with training staff. They have monthly, one-day review meetings and twice-yearly residential meetings.

Employers are beginning to realize that, with the development of computer systems, they have diverse groups of staff who could equally well operate from a home base, with scheduled, but limited, time spent at the office. These potential teleworkers may be in totally different job categories or sectors but are similar in that they make extensive use of computers and VDUs as part of their work, processing and retrieving information. They are not just computer programmers, designers or analysts. There is a wide range of jobs which could be operated in this way. One national branch retailing firm has identified stock management, market research, financial, graphics and design, and customer service jobs as suitable for home-based telework, besides the more conventional areas of computer programming and systems design and development work.

The second group of home-based workers, working exclusively at home, tend to be clerical workers, including data-input and word-processing staff. In a survey of teleworkers undertaken by Ursula Huws in 1984, about 10 per cent of her sample were clerical workers operating at home. This area of telework is probably the least developed in terms of direct employment, but there are growing numbers of self-employed people offering home-based business services. We feel that only if 'back-office' functions of large organizations are widely teleworked, and the workers located in their own homes, will large numbers of people eventually become involved. If this happens, remote working will be transformed from something fairly novel to something fairly commonplace.

However, the less rosy aspect of this is that the totally home-based worker is potentially the most socially isolated, and the people likely to opt for such work, particularly women with domestic responsibilities, tend to make conscious trade-offs between the flexibility of homework and the low paid jobs available. It would be a pity if the potential of the 'new' technology were used to produce a new army of low-paid high-tech outworkers.

Another group who would be predominantly home-based are the disabled, and there are a number of examples of disabled schemes worldwide. Often, disabled people would prefer on-site work, but if that is not feasible, will accept home-based work as an alternative.

Mobile

This is where the car or train, or aeroplane becomes the office. The car, in particular, is often 'the office' for company representatives as well as some senior managers whose jobs involve a lot of travel. It can be equipped with a cellphone, mobile personal computer and even a fax machine.

Equipping company representatives with mobile computers at first sight appears to have little organizational impact, because they are already working remotely. But the overall effects on the organization can be more far-reaching in the long-term.

A large German insurance company with around 20 000 employees, equipped their mobile sales agents with laptop PCs. Data could be transmitted between the PC and the company mainframe, from the agent's home or client's premises. Once the PC was loaded with data, it could be accessed at the customer's premises and used to print out forms and perform calculations. The information flow from head office to mobile employees increased their ability to make better-informed decisions, and they felt themselves to be much more part of the organization, despite their physical remoteness.

As information was increasingly passed direct from agents to head office, one effect was to reduce the role of the regional office. Thus the organization structure could well be simplified, with layers of middle-managers being 'hollowed-out', especially where their previous role was predominantly concerned with information processing.

In this case, the technology was used not in order to reduce costs, but to improve the capacity to compete as a result of better information processing. This seems increasingly to be the motive for introducing more sophisticated information technology. With a mobile, remote workforce, IT can facilitate considerable decentralization of decision making but, at the same time, the head office can retain strong centralized control.

3

What jobs can be teleworked?

The Henley Centre for Forecasting have estimated (1988) that, *if there were no psychological or physical constraints* other than the nature of the job people were doing, almost 50 per cent of employees could be teleworking at least part of the time by 1995. They identified three broad groupings of jobs suitable for remote work.

Group 1: *Professionals*

Those in professional and higher managerial occupations whose work is mainly analytical and self-contained, should theoretically be able to spend a significant amount of time working at home.

Group 2: *Supervisory, routine administrative and sales*

Fairly self-explanatory – their tasks are mainly administrative.

Group 3: *Clerical*

Characterized chiefly by the fact that they process other people's work via a personal computer or word processor. Their tasks are clearly definable, quantifiable and frequently repetitive.

A German study listed 17 areas of work considered suitable for telework:

- word processing
- software documentation
- data-bank information retrieval
- clerical work

- data entry
- translation
- computer programming
- construction (computer-aided design and manufacture)
- writing manuals
- systems analysis
- remote maintenance
- book-keeping
- consultancy
- distance learning/education
- remote control
- estate agency work
- estimation/accounting

We have broken down a list of jobs below into five categories, in order to demonstrate the wide spectrum of jobs which could be teleworked. The list is by no means exhaustive:

1. **Professionals and management specialists:** Architects, accountants, management: marketing, public relations, human resources, finance, etc., financial analysts and brokers.
2. **Professional support workers:** Bookkeepers, translators, proofreaders, indexers, researchers.
3. **'Itinerant' field workers:** Company representatives, surveyors, inspectors, property negotiators, auditors, journalists, insurance brokers.
4. **Information technology specialists:** Systems analysts, software programmers and engineers, etc.
5. **Clerical support workers:** Data entry staff, word processor operators, directory enquiry staff, telesales staff.

All these examples involve the handling, processing or retrieval of information, rather than the production of a tangible 'product', although with the advent of desk-top publishing, the making of books and pamphlets remotely is now fairly common.

The characteristics of suitable jobs

Until now, employers have tended to be very conservative in their perception of which jobs in their organizations are suitable for telework. Figure 4 identifies six characteristics of work and enables a profile of each job to be constructed. From this profile, an assessment of its suitability for telework can be made. In some cases, jobs can be adapted and redesigned to accommodate remote working. This

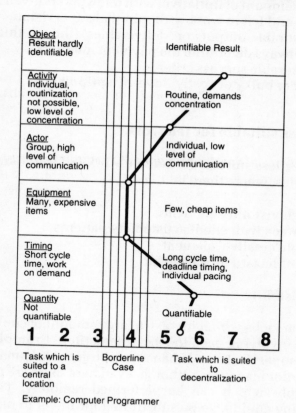

(*Source:* Adapted from Heilmann, 1987; reprinted in Huws et al., 1990.)

Figure IV: *Suitability of tasks for telework*

assessment system was based on the six categories identified by Olson, (1981), from her research in the United
States, and forms the basis for much of the consultancy
work in the area of telework.

In general terms the job should involve:

- a high degree of cerebral, rather than manual, work,
- work done as an individual, or with clearly defined areas of individual work,
- a fair amount of initiative, with teleworkers given objectives and left to work with minimal supervision,
- measurable outputs or 'deliverables' (though this does not always determine the payment method),
- measurable success criteria,
- no very bulky or costly items of equipment.

Jobs less suitable for telework

The jobs less suitable for remote work fall into four main
categories, where there is:

- a high visibility element,
- interface with clients/customers/patients,
- a high 'creative' element
- risk or hazard management.

High visibility

These are jobs which involve a large amount of continuity
work, involving face-to-face interaction. Examples are
office supervisors and managers, project-team managers
and senior managers, although even here there are parts of
such jobs which can be performed remotely. Telecon-
ferencing could also be substituted for travel to meetings
and conferences.

Interface with the public

Where employees' jobs involve personal contact with clients or patients or customers at a central point, obviously telework is not possible. These would include the jobs of receptionists, bank and building society counter staff, hospital nurses, retail assistants and checkout staff, public transport staff, teachers, lecturers, and canteen staff. In the long term, however, changes in work organization could further increase the scope of telework, for example the growth of distance learning, home banking and teleshopping.

Creativity

Jobs which include a considerable creative element, where ideas need to be 'bounced off' other people, are more difficult to operate well remotely, especially for home-based workers. Catherine Simmons, a home-based author of computer-based training programmes for Commercial Union Assurance, comments that a lack of creative stimulation can be a serious drawback, and that sometimes she and her on-site colleagues develop similar ideas and 're-invent the wheel'. However, if the job can be operated mainly on-site, or if the need for communication with others can be 'batched' and undertaken regularly at a central point, these problems can be overcome, to a certain extent. But there is really no substitute for interaction with other human beings face-to-face to stimulate the creative function.

Managing risk

Where jobs are involved with situations of risk, for example certain aspects of environmental health officers' duties, there is a vital need for colleagues to meet face-to-face to draw on and learn from each others' experience. Though this would make remote work more problematic, a system of regular face-to-face meetings could be arranged for teleworkers, and ideas could also be exchanged by electronic mail systems.

4

Advantages and drawbacks of telework to the user organization

In this chapter, the pluses and minuses of telework will be discussed, from the viewpoint of the user organization. The principal potential advantages of telework to the organization are:

- productivity gains,
- reduction of overhead costs,
- retention of rare skills,
- penetration of unusual labour market sources.

The principal potential disadvantages to the organization are:

- lack of commitment to organizational goals and culture,
- problems of communication and supervision.

Productivity gains

There have been some startling claims made about the productivity gains of telework, particularly the home-based variety. These claims range from 30 per cent to as high as 100 per cent. Exaggerated claims should be treated with a measure of scepticism and probably stem from four main factors:

1. Work-at-home means that time spent travelling to and from work may well be translated into working-time. This is not a productivity gain per hour, but a lengthening of time worked.
2. Working at home avoids many of the distractions of working on-site, such as coffee-breaks, chats and so on.

21

At the office, informal breaks are part of the working-day: at home, breaks to undertake domestic chores do not count as work time. The amount of distraction experienced at home also depends on the suitability of the home setting.

3. Sometimes the payment system for teleworkers closely links pay and performance, which means that employers are not paying for unproductive time.

4. Huws (1984) feels there may be a 'Hawthorne effect' among pilot teleworkers (i.e. because they are being closely studied and monitored, their behaviour and performance may be favourably affected). This might not be sustained if the work pattern becomes more routine.

Even where a teleworker is not paid by results, but is on a salary for example, there is still an emphasis on output, or 'deliverable' segments of work, to a much greater extent than with on-site staff. This is in essence inevitable with a remote form of work supervision, compared to the traditional 'over-the-shoulder' method, and this may lead to an over-emphasis on the quantifiable aspects of the work carried out by teleworkers.

In some telework schemes, improvements in productivity form part of the case for introducing home-based working, but can turn out to be over-optimistic because of unforeseen consequences of the new working pattern. Texaco home-based staff as well as Training Agency Inspectors found that they had to spend a higher than expected amount of time performing routine administrative tasks and, in the latter case, this has led to modifications in the scheme. The productivity gains expected may take some time to be fulfilled. Also, once teleworkers become more skilled at using their equipment, the time expended on routine administration may fall. This emphasizes the need for training in the use of the computer equipment *before* schemes are implemented.

Reductions in overhead costs

Employers' traditional reasons for using homeworkers or outworkers have always included the reduction of overhead costs, since usually the costs of heating, lighting and repair were transferred to the individual worker. The trend recently among responsible employers is to give allowances to their teleworkers to cover these costs, which we would advocate as good practice. There is still a significant net cost reduction to employers, in most cases.

Cutting overhead costs, particularly office costs, was an important aspect of the Rank Xerox networking scheme. In 1981 they investigated the costs of employing workers in Central London. These findings would also be similar for employers in high-cost areas around London and other parts of the 'Golden Triangle'. The costs were found to be:

- facilities including rent, rates, depreciation, maintenance, energy, security — 31%
- salaries — 30%
- employment costs including National Insurance contributions, company pension, benefit contributions — 15%
- data processing, travel, miscellaneous — 24%

They found that around one third of employment costs were office facility costs. These, because they are spread between many budgets, tend to be hidden or considered as a taken-for-granted cost which is fixed and not amenable to reduction. Rank Xerox were able, through their networking initiative, to dispose of a small London office building, which they consider was easier to re-let than a large one (large offices often tend to be left empty after wholesale relocation).

Huws, Korte and Robinson (1990) point out that savings in overhead costs will not follow merely from allowing some staff to work from home part of the time – it is only where part or all of a building can be vacated or sub-let that

real savings stand to be made. Judkins, West and Drew
(1985) of Rank Xerox also feel that telework might enable
a business to continue to use a small premises whilst
expanding its workforce. Certainly, employers have
turned to telework as a way of rationalizing office usage, or
avoiding a move to larger premises, or building annexes
and extensions to existing premises. In all these cases it
could be argued that telework enables cost savings to be
made.

Many companies or organizations considering decen-
tralizing work may wish to retain an office, however small,
in a prestige location, because of the positive image it
creates among clients, customers and the general public.
Also it provides an easy interface point with the outside
world and can accommodate the 'strategic core' of the
organization. In terms of employee motivation, however,
the Rank Xerox managers felt that a smart office environment was not a motivator to better performance but was
really only a 'hygiene factor'. This thinking is in line with
the work of Frederick Herzberg, who argued that the work
environment needs to be of a sufficient minimum standard
so as to avoid worker dissatisfaction (in the same way that
good hygiene avoids disease) but, however good, will not
provide the positive motivating force required to improve
peoples' work performance.

Retaining scarce skills

Even during periods of recession, employers continue to
suffer shortages in certain skill areas. An advantage of
telework is that it can be put into practice in a way which
gives employees autonomy and flexibility as to how and
where their work is performed. This can help to retain
people in skill-shortage occupations or those with particular skills who could not be employed in a conventional
manner.

It can also help to keep valued workers who would

otherwise leave when, for example, one partner in a household takes a job in a new location necessitating a house move. The employer of the other partner could retain that employee by using telework. A further example is that of retaining women employees after maternity leave. Telework can be tailored to meet their needs, and may avoid losing their skills entirely.

An example of both is Catherine Simmons, of Commercial Union, who moved house *and* started a family. Her unique skills in designing computer-based training programmes were extremely difficult to replace, and it was agreed that she could work part-time at home after a short period of maternity leave, a pattern which appears to be working very successfully.

In government departments and local authorities, telework is being used to find ways of providing services more effectively by retaining skilled staff. In many cases, public service organizations have to recruit in geographical areas characterized by tight labour markets, and are often not able to match remuneration levels on offer in the private sector. They are also currently having difficulties in revenue collection, but at the same time face public pressure for increased efficiency and levels of provision. It is perhaps not surprising that the local authorities considering telework as an option are concentrated, by and large, in London and the South-East.

One example is Kent County Council, which is beginning to use unorthodox working arrangements to retain valuable skills. For instance, a training manager in the information systems department works partly in the office and partly at home in order to combine work with family demands. Whilst she admits that combining the two roles can be stressful, she is pleased to be able to continue to undertake a responsible and valued job. Employers can combine telework and on-site work as well as field-work in endless permutations to suit individual and organizational needs. Arrangements can span a period of several months or years, in some cases eventually leading to a return to conventional on-site, full-time working. Telework does not have to involve a permanent move to work at home.

Where employers were using telework in order to retain scarce skills, Huws Korte and Robinson (1990) found that the teleworkers involved had a relatively strong bargaining position, and often had considerable influence in determining how work was arranged. Typical jobs were computer professionals, consultants and writers.

Attracting unusual sources of labour

Although telework has the potential to open up new labour sources, for example among people with young children or elderly dependants, older workers or the disabled, these sources remain largely untapped as yet. Telework schemes tend to be aimed, at the moment, either at existing members of a company's workforce, or alternatively, at accessing cheaper labour sources by means of setting up satellite offices.

Exceptions to this general trend are the two well-known schemes in the UK for computer professionals. Both CPS/ICL and FI Group were originally set up to access women workers with IT skills who, because of domestic responsibilities (usually young children), had left full-time work. Remote work for this group has become something of a tradition over the last 25 years, although 'clones' of the idea have been few.

In terms of back-office functions, schemes to access the potential home-based workforce are only just beginning, Typing Plus being an example. They report no difficulty in recruiting staff to work at home often by word-of-mouth on a self-employed basis, at lower rates of pay than on-site staff. A recruitment advertisement for proofreaders recently produced 200 responses from qualified people. There is no doubt that a pent-up demand exists particularly from women eager to be able to work. They are seeking jobs offering hours which fit in with their children's needs, which enable them to work either away from home, or within the home.

The other group which features in telework schemes is the disabled. Often the schemes involve training in information technology skills such as word-processing, database work and accounting, and in some cases schemes are initiated by charitable groups, and supported by State or EC funding. After training, disabled people are placed into suitable jobs with interested employers. American Express (USA) and Control Data Corporation are two American examples where the disabled are home (or hospital)-trained and placed into positions within the organization.

Reservations about such disabled schemes have included the view that they are an excuse not to rehabilitate the disabled into an office setting, which would avoid the social isolation of remote work. Certainly on-site work for the disabled, which many disabled people would prefer, has never been vigorously pursued in the UK. When surveyed, disabled teleworkers want companionship and opportunities to meet new people, which are difficult to bring about if people are working at home.

The IT World project on developing home training for the disabled in the UK has demonstrated that such training is viable, and trainees can reach a standard suitable for employment, but like several such schemes, when money ran out, it was terminated. A Netherlands project, to set up a commercially independent enterprise using telework for the disabled, foundered because it lost the most able participants.

The International Labour Organisation has commented that these experiments face a particular dilemma: to successfully operate in a commercial environment it is necessary to recruit the most able human resources, which is often not consistent with the goal of helping groups with more severe disablement problems.

However, given consistent funding and support, the

case studies prove that telework can be a viable alternative for many categories of disabled people, and social isolation can be avoided in some cases by basing the work in neighbourhood centres, as has been done by Empirica in various European countries.

Other disadvantaged groups who could be offered employment through telework are:

- carers,
- the long-term unemployed,
- people in hospitals,
- people in nursing homes,
- people in prisons.

There is one example of specially selected women prisoners in the United States who process bookings for a chain of hotels, enabling them to learn keyboard skills and to earn some money to support their families. Given the lack of meaningful work available to prisoners, this may be an area worth exploring in the UK.

Problems of commitment to organizational goals and culture

The fostering within employing organizations of shared goals and values, and the development of 'corporate culture' is a current pre-occupation among managers. In Peter's and Waterman's popular book, *In Search of Excellence* (1982), which studied America's most successful companies, one of the factors highlighted was a dominant and coherent corporate culture which was understood and acted upon by all levels of employee within the organization, and which influenced their day-to-day actions. In the context of remote work or telework, the obvious problem is a lack of face-to-face contact leading to the failure to internalize attitudes, values and behaviour, which are often absorbed through informal messages at work.

This is perhaps not a problem where a teleworker has worked for an organization for a considerable length of time, when he or she would be assumed to have already 'internalized' the correct way of doing things. The problem may arise where teleworkers are recruited from the external labour market, or are transformed into remote workers soon after recruitment. The Digital Equipment Company (DEC) have identified corporate culture as one possible problem of homeworking, as they pride themselves on having a well-developed set of shared values. FI Group try to inculcate their corporate culture by means of a Charter outlining the goals and values of the organization, and CPS/ICL has a Mission Statement, the content of which is made clear to all recruits.

The main responsibility for socializing remote workers is bound to fall to the direct line manager, who would have the most regular contact with them. It may be considered as particularly important for 'itinerants' or field-workers who are often the only contact that clients and customers have with the organization. Their 'ambassadorial' role is a particularly crucial one as they are the 'front-line' communicators of the organization's 'corporate image'. Adequate training for field teleworkers in interpersonal skills, especially at the induction stage, is vital. Training could be given on-site, or delivered by distance-learning methods, depending upon the particular circumstances.

Problems of communication and supervision

The perceived problem of managing teleworkers is perhaps the greatest barrier to its wider application. Empirica's survey of European managers found that worries about the extra costs and resources felt necessary to supervise remote work were a major reason for rejecting it. However, in case studies of firms already using telework, problems of supervision tended to diminish over time, though most admitted that at the implementation stage extra inputs from various specialist managerial functions were needed.

Better communications systems are becoming more crucial in the 'distributed' or 'flexible' organization or 'adhocracy' which is seen by some management commentators to be the typical structural form of the future. Sheila Rothwell (1987) feels that the need to develop appropriate styles of communication for these 'flexi-workers' is going to be a difficult challenge for managers. Most managers are used to operating an 'over-the-shoulder' mode of supervision and derive much of their status from the size of their 'visible' workforce. Some supervisors even find it difficult to adapt to the demands of managing part-timers — employees on half-time or even four-fifths time contracts complain that they are excluded from day-to-day information networks.

Rank Xerox made a particular effort in this regard with their 'networker' scheme by giving each networker a manager or 'mentor' who was responsible for company communication, as well as being included on circulation lists, company directories, and invited to functions and meetings. Digital also have managers whose particular job it is to look after their teleworking staff.

Teleworkers need ongoing support and reassurance from their managers, and this is likely to take the form of telephone interaction or in future by video-computer links. There is nothing worse for remote workers than feeling completely cut off from their employing organization, and there are obvious dangers in this of demotivation and demoralization. Managers need to make extra and sustained efforts to include remote staff in corporate life.

The type and nature of remote supervision may be affected by:

- the nature of the work,
- the status and knowledge of the teleworker,
- the organizational culture and tradition.

The main problem is the transition from the 'over-the-shoulder' mode of supervision to what the Rank Xerox managers call 'output mode'. This involves a move to judgement by results alone, rather than a close involvement in how the work is done. More directional styles may be adopted by managers of lower-status employees or those who are trainees or new to telework which will obviously be time-consuming. More delegation may be allowed to highly experienced or qualified staff, with the manager able to trust the teleworker to complete a task and ask for assistance if necessary. That is why most of the pilot schemes involve staff of several years' standing, who are also positively motivated towards remote work.

There seems to be a tradition of close supervision in the case of computer professionals working remotely, even though the staff are high-status, well-qualified and motivated. Both FI and CPS/ICL staff have their work broken down into short time-segments, and the FI management hierarchy has a high number of levels. This may reflect organizational culture, but another factor may be the nature of the work, which can suffer from considerable cost overruns without close control.

Many managers may not be experienced in setting clear objectives and time scales, let alone specifying the various resource inputs necessary, although with the growth of subcontraction of services within organizations, there may be a growing area of expertise which could be tapped.

Sometimes in situations of ambiguity or novelty or fear of loss of control, the reaction among managers is to over-formalize the style of supervision, which can itself lead to dissatisfaction among teleworkers. Managers may need to strike a delicate balance between too much and too little supervision of remote staff (see also Chapter 11).

Case studies: two women teleworkers

1. _The career-bridge teleworker_

Jane Adams has been working from home for a business services company since she was pregnant with her first baby some two years ago. She had particularly valuable computer-based skills which were hard to replace:

> At the time there were some misgivings in my firm about allowing me to work from home – it was completely new territory for them as they hadn't done it before. In fact they did get as far as advertising for a replacement for me, but no-one suitable applied, so it was decided to allow me to become a remote worker.
>
> I now work for the most part at home, making occasional visits to the London central office, which I look forward to. Other than that I have very good links with my boss and colleagues through electronic mail and, of course, the telephone as well. At the moment I work part-time, but I am building up my hours as my daughter gets older.
>
> I would eventually like to return to office-based work when my family is complete but, at present, this is really the only viable option. From my point of view, if I had left my job completely it would have been difficult to get back on board because of all the rapid changes in my field – I'd have been left behind.
>
> The good thing about telework is that I can work without any hassle, and I can combine keeping an eye on domestic things with concentrating on my work. When I first started working this way I did find it hard to separate the two, and would find myself thinking about one while doing the other – you have to sort that out fairly quickly or you're lost.
>
> In my opinion, telework can't be done without proper childcare. Certainly in my work I couldn't have a toddler around me or just work when the baby is asleep. I happen to have someone who comes to me, but you could operate by taking the child to a minder or nursery too. I think the money I pay for this is well-worthwhile but, of course, I am relatively well-paid.
>
> You have to have the right personality for this work –

conscientious and well-organized. It wouldn't work otherwise. There has to be a high level of trust between you and your boss too, and good relations with colleagues. I think I've got that. I sometimes get lonely, but that's really something you just have to accept. If you're a woman who wants company after being at home with young children, I wouldn't recommend this form of work.

All-in-all, I regard myself as privileged in being able to carry on doing the job I enjoy in a way that fits in with my personal circumstances. I also feel like a pioneer in a way — there's a lot riding on how successfully this works out. If it is seen as a good idea then I don't doubt that there are other women who will get the opportunity to work in this way.

2. *The woman returner*

Elaine Trevor has been employed part-time by a firm in a nearby small town as a home-based word-processor for several months now. Her work is delivered to her house on audio-tape or paper, and the completed documents are sent back by means of a modem link to the office to be printed out.

I have three school-age children, and I do the work when they are at school. I keep a log of the hours I work each week and that's how I get paid. Once I have taken the youngest child to school I can work undisturbed. There are no set hours but I have to send back the work on time and to a good level of quality. The company provided me with a personal computer, desk, chair, modem and so on, and I work from my dining-room during the day. Except for the courier who delivers the work and an occasional query to my supervisor over the telephone, I don't get any contact with my employers — I don't need to visit the office at all. That suits me really — what I wanted was some means of earning money and a job which fits in with my children.

I did apply for jobs in the newspaper which offered hours fitting in with the children — clerical work in a school for example — but I had no joy. Apparently they get about eighty or ninety replies in this area for any job like that, so there's obviously a lot of women with young families out there, like me, who are looking for work.

I worked in a Building Society office before I had my family and learned my basic skills there. It was just a question of updating my word-processing skills and learning a new package when I got this job. The main advantage is that I don't have to travel to work, it's here waiting for me and it's pretty straightforward.

I tend to get given the more routine, non-urgent correspondence to deal with. The urgent letters and documents are dealt with in the office, so the firm still employs word-processors there, as well as secretaries to the top managers, of course. They guarantee me a minimum level of work each week, and so far there doesn't seem to be a shortage.

I see this job as suiting me at the moment. Pretty soon my youngest child will be more independent and then I might look for an office job, possibly full-time or maybe a term-time contract – if I can find one. I think employers are just starting to think about employing women like me in different ways, other than the traditional part-timer. My company has several teleworkers like me – and the local authority up the road has got quite a number doing data input work, keeping track of changes of address as a result of the poll-tax, though of course that might disappear in a year or two when the new property-based tax comes in.

5

Advantages and drawbacks of telework to the individual

This chapter discusses the pluses and minuses of telework, from the vantage point of the individual teleworker.

The principal advantages of telework to the individual are:

- autonomy and increased job satisfaction,
- freedom from time constraints,
- bridging the 'career gap',
- a better balance between work and home-life,
- cutting or eliminating commuting costs and time.

The principal disadvantages of telework to the individual are:

- poorer pay and fringe benefits,
- can create conflicts between work and home-life,
- can lead to social isolation,
- increases routine tasks,
- leads to career marginalization.

Autonomy and increased job satisfaction

There is considerable choice for employers in the way that telework is organized. Much of the research into the impact on teleworkers has shown that the groups which report the greatest positive benefits are generally managerial, professional and technical staff. Huws, Korte and Robinson's survey (1990) of existing telework schemes in Europe found consistently high satisfaction levels with all aspects of their working-life amongst remote workers.

Although they attempted to compensate for this, their sample tended to be biased towards highly qualified staff.

From the available research, it appears that the most popular working mode among teleworkers is the combination of home and office work, where staff have a home workstation but also retain opportunities to interact with colleagues at the workplace. This tends to bestow flexibility and avoid the feelings of isolation from corporate life which arise from totally home-based work.

One of Olson's studies (1981) of American teleworkers, most of whom were well-qualified males, found that their on-site autonomy was not diminished when they became teleworkers. Whether remote workers who do *not* have scarce skills would be given similar opportunities to shape their own work-life is more questionable.

Freedom from time constraints

Theoretically, telework can offer the freedom to work whatever hours suit the individual as long as the work is completed on time and to an acceptable standard. However, with directly employed teleworkers, there is sometimes a tendency among supervisory management to expect their remote subordinates to continue to work conventional hours (and some teleworkers may still prefer to do so). Lotte Bailyn (1988), an American psychologist, cites a British personnel manager who was very willing to let his staff work at home, but admitted that, if there were a Test Match in session, he would be tempted to check on whether the employee was working! This attitude can undermine the potential time-flexibility of telework. There is some evidence, however, to indicate that this is changing.

Teleworkers making extensive use of computer networks, mainframe support staff for example, need to perform work when the computer is not in daily use, which means outside office hours. Other types of job, where extensive interaction with office-based staff is necessary, or where site visits are an integral part of the job, will mean that remote workers will continue to need to work fairly conventional hours.

For women teleworkers with domestic responsibilities – usually young children – flexibility tends to mean something rather different. Ursula Huws's 1984 survey of teleworkers, almost all of whom were women, found that more than half felt flexibility, or convenience, was important, plus the fact that their work could be fitted around their primary commitment to home and family. There is a lot of evidence that this group work very early in the mornings or late at night and sometimes even through the night in order to complete their work without disrupting home life. Flexibility in this more negative context means the ability to hold down some kind of job, often part-time and, in the case of women computer professionals, to keep up their skills in a rapidly changing environment, whilst bringing up a family.

Bridging the career gap

Evidence from local authority, oil industry and retail sector case studies shows that remote work is already being used on a limited scale to avoid a career break for women after statutory maternity leave. For the employer, this means retaining valued employees: for the teleworker it can often mean some continuity of earnings, as well as a chance to remain on the career ladder of the organization, and to keep up-to-date with skills, which otherwise would rapidly become redundant.

Increasingly, financial pressures are leading families to adopt a dual-income strategy and labour-force statistics show women are returning to some form of paid work much sooner than previously. Just under half of women with pre-school age children do some form of paid work according to Department of Employment figures, and the evidence points to a greater participation on the part of this group in the labour-force in the future if opportunities are made available to them.

Telework could provide one option among many for employers wishing to retain valued female staff. Alternatives include:

- workplace nursery provision,
- long-term career-break schemes,
- flexible working hours,
- assistance with childcare costs.

None of these are as yet widespread in the UK. Employers still only usually choose the telework option if it fits with the particular circumstances, including the type of work involved, how valuable retention of the particular employee/s is considered to be, and if it is congruent with the particular strategies and culture of the employing organization. Career-gap telework is still in its infancy and, even in the telecommunications industry itself where there is obviously familiarity with the hardware, examples are still surprisingly limited.

Balancing work and home life

A lot of writing on the future of work has concentrated on the positive benefits of remote work for people wishing to make a fuller contribution to family life, to see more of their children and to develop their participation in local community life. For example, this group is discussed by James Robertson in his book *Future Work* (1985). He calls them 'lifestyle entrepreneurs' who want to maximize freedom and 'do their own thing'. As well as telework, he points to the growth of part-time work, self-employment and early retirement as part of the trend towards 'own-work', which enables people to involve themselves in voluntary work, become househusbands or adopt a more self-sufficient lifestyle, substituting their own unpaid work to provide for some of their own needs, for work in the formal economy.

Charles Handy calls this the 'portfolio lifestyle'. Alvin Toffler (1981) is similarly optimistic about the effects of returning work into the home, predicting lower divorce rates, a more egalitarian sharing of tasks between partners, and stronger community ties. As with some of the claims of higher productivity among teleworkers, such predictions are perhaps best treated with an element of scepticism.

There is certainly a group of teleworkers who self-select for such a work pattern. For example, subscribers to 'Own-base', a bi-monthly newsletter for home-based workers, tend to be very positive about their choice of lifestyle. They have a prior orientation towards such attitudes, but what limited evidence there is points to them being a predominantly self-employed grouping. The majority of directly employed teleworkers will not be 'portfolio people', but have similar aspirations to other groups, or they may well have little choice in the matter of their work pattern.

There appears as yet to be little if any hard empirical evidence that telework *causes* an improvement in family life, equality between the sexes or a greater commitment to the local community. The ability to successfully combine work and home life in one location is much more contingent on the situation of the individual teleworker.

The factors which affect this include:

- having suitable separate work accommodation,
- being able to concentrate fully on work or domestic life as necessary,
- being able to negotiate an unwritten 'contract' with family and friends about working time,
- having a good relationship with partner, wife or husband.

The disadvantages of combining work and home life will be discussed later in this chapter.

Reducing time and costs of commuting

In theory, teleworkers can live in their preferred location and substitute electronic communication for physical travel. They can reduce their living costs by moving to cheaper housing areas, or improve their quality of life in the countryside, and save on travel cost, stresses and time.

The amount of time and costs saved will depend upon what type of work teleworkers do. Only a proportion of future teleworkers are likely to be entirely home-based: others will combine office and homeworking. Travel costs might be reduced but not totally eliminated. Some will be field-workers where travel to clients' premises would still be required, meaning that travel costs would be relatively unaffected.

Staff often value a reduction in the stress of commuting, especially if they have to use the more notorious commuter rail-routes or crowded road-routes. Some who already work from home appreciate the ability to start work straight away without wasting time in travelling. Other people value the 'psychological space' which commuting gives them, an enforced separation between home and arrival at the office. One home-based worker we encountered put on a coat and walked around the block before coming back in and starting work – he literally 'walked to work'.

As far as a more dispersed workforce is concerned, with more teleworkers living in remote, rural areas, there is little evidence to date that this will happen on a massive scale. The Highlands and Islands scheme, jointly funded by British Telecom and the Highlands and Islands Development Board and the European Community which is due to open in 1991, will provide a digital network in the area five to eight years before other rural areas of Britain. It is designed to attract businesses as well as to encourage rural telework. The evidence to date is that many future teleworkers may be clustered relatively near to their employers who may be based in larger towns such as Inverness, although with better marketing of their services nationally, self-employed teleworkers are really location-independent. Future teleworkers are probably more likely to be suburban than rural dwellers, despite the preponderance of Arcadian country cottages which feature in the marketing of telework.

Huws, Korte and Robinson (1990) point out that broadband optical-fibre cable networks, which would facilitate telework, are very expensive, and unlikely to become available to most rural homes, and also that a movement to rural living may in fact actually *increase* travel by private car, to the detriment of public transport, because rural areas have very poor (or increasingly non-existent) public transport networks.

Poorer pay and fringe benefits

There is evidence from surveys of homeworkers and teleworkers that:

- self-employed teleworkers tend to earn less than those who are employed, and also have no fringe benefits,
- data-processing professionals earn less than their on-site counterparts,
- people who work at home as a positive choice (usually men) generally have higher earnings,
- people who are restricted to work-at-home (usually women) generally have the lowest earnings,
- female teleworkers tend to be second-earners in the household, and often trade pay for flexibility.

Brocklehurst (1989) feels that the on-site differentiation between workers, in terms of skill, status, gender and pay are being paralleled among new-technology home-workers.

We feel that there are basically three broad groups of teleworkers:

1. well-paid, employed, highly qualified, mostly male teleworkers who often combine office and home-work,
2. an intermediate group of less well-paid, but highly qualified, mostly female computer-professionals,
3. poorly paid, often self-employed, mostly female teleworkers, who tend to work entirely at home.

Potential conflicts between work and home life

Telework can resolve conflicts between home and work life, as discussed in a previous section, but it can also exacerbate them. Over the last two hundred years home and work life have become increasingly separated for most people, and the 'home' remains the psychological domain of the woman, despite women's increasing participation in the formal economy. This can lead to women feeling that their 'territory' is being 'invaded', if their partner becomes home-based.

Employees may also resist the home move because of the persistence of the low status and sweated-labour image of traditional manufacturing homework, and this perception may also affect the behaviour of friends and relatives. One teleworker we interviewed said that visitors to the house often did not take her home employment seriously and she suffered from constant interruptions as a result.

It is very much down to the individual teleworker to impose a separation between work and domestic responsibilities, which takes a good deal of will-power and determination. One home-based computerized book-keeper reported that he always puts on a tie and dresses smartly to denote that work-time has started. At the other end of the day, a homeworker complained that 'no-one blows a whistle at 5 o'clock so you just carry on working'. Some of the Training Standards Inspectors reported that they sometimes felt guilty when they were at home but not working, even during leisure hours.

Women who are combining paid work and childcare

obviously have a particular difficulty in separating the conflicting pressures, which can lead to working unsocial hours, and the noise of a young family can be disruptive to concentration even if they are being supervised by someone else. Lotte Bailyn (1988) feels that it may be easier for women than men to work at home – they do it all the time – but, paradoxically, it may be easier for men to avoid its distractions and give work the necessary priority while at home.

There is also evidence that conflicts will be exacerbated if relationships at home are already poor or one partner is not in sympathy with the other working at home. Family circumstances or attitudes may sometimes create additional stresses, not lessen them.

Social isolation

More than 60 per cent of Huws's (1984) respondents, and over half of the Training Standards Inspectors thought that the major drawback of working at home was the feeling of isolation, despite monthly meetings and training sessions in the latter case. Catherine Simmons, a home-based computer professional feels that day-to-day loneliness is a feature of teleworking, although her work at home is supplemented by visits to her employer, telephone contacts and people visiting her home on business. For totally home-based workers, the isolation would be even more profound.

Huws, Korte and Robinson (1990) feel that social isolation is the greatest deterrent to full-time home-based telework, and increases the attractions of combined office and remote work. Only a minority of people will settle for entirely home-based work, and this is reflected in their survey of interest in telework, which found that the greatest level of acceptability was in households with young children where alternative options are limited. Even among previously highly committed teleworkers and authors on the subject such as Tom Forester (1989), disillusion with home-based work can set in after a couple of years. He reports that of five friends working in a similar way, two became divorced, one became seriously depressed and another returned to on-site work. Only one stuck to telework.

Norma Whitcombe, a founder member of the Society of Freelance Editors and Proofreaders, feels that many people do not think sufficiently about the issue of isolation when they start working at home, but many get no social contact except over the telephone. 'You need to enjoy your own company and it isn't a form of work for the sort of woman who goes back to work in search of social contact', she comments.

What many teleworkers lack is the opportunity to talk informally with peers about the latest developments or problems within the job. This is a particular drawback where teleworkers are recruited from the external labour market, and have limited opportunities to really get to know their colleagues or to gain an insight into the structure and roles of the organization of which they are a part. That is why good induction training for this type of employee is so crucial.

Employers of teleworkers can adopt a number of strategies to minimize social isolation:

- always use volunteers as teleworkers,
- use home/office combinations or mobile work instead of totally home-based telework,
- use telework flexibly over short periods of time rather than permanently,
- allow teleworkers access to electronic mail systems which facilitate peer contact,
- set up networks (such as Rank Xerox's Xanadu) to provide a focus for information and an opportunity to meet from time-to-time,
- give teleworkers training in self-management skills, similar to those appropriate to people starting self-employment,
- set up neighbourhood work centres for remote workers,

- set up satellite offices rather than home-based telework.

There is no doubt that home-based telework will tend to isolate people from the social and political life of the workplace, and removes a support system from the individual. From studies of unemployment, work is seen to give the individual:

- a time structure to the working day,
- contacts and experiences outside the immediate family,
- status and social identity,
- a consciousness of working for a collectivity.

Many, or all of these factors may be absent with some forms of remote work.

Increase in routine tasks

One of the support systems which on-site work can provide for technical, managerial and professional staff is clerical back-up. Telework of the home-based variety tends to push the responsibility for routine tasks of this kind back on to the individual, and there may be fears that this may 'swamp' the teleworker, preventing him or her from accomplishing the important key objectives of the job.

Texaco field professionals who were moved to home-based work feared that requests for feedback from their superiors would become a priority and the 'real work' would suffer.

A surprising number of employees 'transformed' into teleworkers were not given adequate prior training in keyboard and word-processing skills, or the training tended to be given on a 'blanket' basis taking no account of what level of competence the individuals had already attained. Good training would enable remote workers to attain a sufficient skill level to help to minimize the time taken over routine tasks.

The Empirica telework survey found that their sample of teleworkers were demanding to have their own fax or photocopying machines at home. Unless they would be in constant use, employers were reluctant to provide these, because it was not felt to be cost-effective to do so. In some cases, teleworkers could use commercial office services in their local area, although this would itself tend to be costly if used on a large scale. The economics of providing these machines as part of the home workstation may change as the price comes down, and employers may feel that the advantages of providing a comprehensive communications system to teleworkers may outweigh the cost drawbacks.

Career marginalization

Teleworkers, in particular the home-based variety, tend to suffer from a lack of visibility, and often have legitimate fears of being marginalized from the internal career ladder of the employing organization. This is not so marked among those who work partly in the office and partly away from it.

Many teleworkers (especially women) work part-time and are therefore doubly disadvantaged because part-time work is often not considered by many employers to qualify employees for career advancement. It is vital to differentiate here between the different groupings of teleworkers. The technical, managerial and professional grouping will probably have strong expectations of continuing to enjoy long-term career development. Clerical support teleworkers, like their on-site equivalents, would be in relatively 'careerless' occupations with very limited opportunities for promotion.

Among the high-status grouping, teleworkers fall into two main categories which may affect how their development is perceived:

- individuals who may telework whereas most of their colleagues in that job category do not,
- complete groupings or job categories who *all* work remotely.

The first category may in fact be more disadvantaged in career terms, unless the employer takes steps to include them fully in the development process. The second category would be more likely to have self-contained training and development processes, similar to those of the sales function of an organization, for example, whereby field sales staff have opportunities to climb the managerial ladder.

Olson (1981) believes that in America, promotability in many organizations has a lot more to do with visibility than with performance linked to some objective criteria and, although inefficient, this attitude is very entrenched and changes slowly. If this attitude is also true of the UK, it is obviously to the disadvantage of employees who work remotely.

Case studies: two views of home and work

1. *Home, sweet home?*

'I'm just off to the shops', John's wife calls out from the hall, 'I'll see you later'.

John, meanwhile, sits in front of his blank computer screen. 'Oh, God!', he murmurs to himself, 'just getting started on this report is the worst part . . . perhaps if I just key in a couple of opening sentences it'll make me feel better'. He sits for a while and keys in a few words. 'It's no good, I'll make myself a coffee and then try again.'

John is a dual-location market researcher who, by agreement with his boss, spends blocks of time at home doing market analysis work on his computer. Initially, the idea of not having to travel relentlessly in to work every day of the working year had appealed greatly but, after only a few months, he was beginning to go off the idea.

John makes himself a coffee and then guiltily strolls down the back garden for a cigarette. Returning to the house, he opens the fridge and lingers awhile nibbling at bits and pieces. He finally returns to his study and sits back in front of his computer with a sigh.

Suddenly the telephone rings. 'Ah!, relief at last', thinks John, eager to feel that he is doing something useful. Alas, it is a wrong number – his number is similar to that of the local mini-cab firm.

'I think I will ring Norman, he's always good for a chat'. John rings his familiar number from memory. 'Hello Norm, it's John here doing what passes for work. How are things with you, got time to talk? . . . I've just completed the field-work research for a marketing report but I'm having a block with the writing-up. Deadline is the end of this week, but it's hard to be strict with yourself when you are at home – there's no sense of urgency.'

After a few minutes conversation and commiseration, John puts the telephone down and resumes his work. He hears the front door bang. 'I'm back', says John's wife, 'How are you getting on with your write-up?'

'Oh, fine!', he lied, 'making good progress'. After another long pause, he looks down at his watch. 'Reckon I'll go for a walk around the block to clear my head and perhaps take in a quick drink and snack at the pub'. Suddenly he heard his wife's voice over his shoulder: 'you don't look to have done very much dear'. 'Oh, don't nag, I think I deserve a break . . . the walk might inspire me'.

An hour and a half later, John returned from his 'local'. 'I thought you were only going for a little while', complained his wife. 'Well, I met Jim there – he's always good company. Some local worthy tried to drag me into helping organize this year's fête . . . went on and on about it.'

'I hope you didn't say yes!'

'No, I didn't. Some people think that, just because you are at home some of the time, you haven't got a proper job. Anyway, it's fatal getting dragged into these local community things – they just swallow up time and you can never escape once you're in the net.'

Back at his PC, John resumes his struggle for the inspiration required to launch his report. He thinks: 'Perhaps I'll drop into the office tomorrow and write it up there. I'm not supposed to be in until Friday, but I'm sure no-one will mind. I can catch up on all the office gossip too. There are supposed to be few distractions at home but I find it hard to really get down to work here – there is no sense of urgency and it's difficult to get into gear – it's so boring. On the other hand, the first day of the Test Match will be on television tomorrow. Perhaps I will stay out of the office until Friday. Damn, I've just run out of cigarettes . . .'

2. The anachronistic office?

Erica returns from a day at the office. She is working out a six-month contract for a public relations firm based in a nearby town. Previously she has been working from home for several years on project-based contracts for various firms.

Her partner Tom asks her what sort of day she has had. 'The traffic was awful as usual. I can't wait to get back here to work. It's like going back to the Dark Ages working in an office.'

'Why's that? Surely it's nice to have company instead of being on your own here?'

'Company? All they seem to talk about is boring office politics all the time – or who's having an affair with whom. They can't understand how you can actually get work done at home, and assume that you must miss all the little power games that get acted out at work . . . some people can't live without that sort of thing I suppose.'

'One of the reasons I decided to work at home was precisely in order to avoid some of the people I came across in offices – it's amazing how they lose sight of what they're supposed to be working towards. The office politics takes priority over the firm's objectives – or that's how it seems to me.'

'Well', said Tom, 'they do say that when it comes to "getting on" in a career, who you know matters as much as – or sometimes more – than what you know, or how well you perform in a job.'

Erica pauses: 'Yes, it's the quality of your work that must be most important when you work away from the office –

that's really mainly how you are judged. Mind you, there's
always some contact, by telephone and the odd meeting, so
you've got to know how to present yourself and get on with
other people too.'

'The other thing that really gets me', says Erica when
they are sitting down to supper, 'is the sheer amount of
time people waste at work. I wouldn't dream of charging
my time for some of the things they get paid for – making
dental appointments and doing the crossword. One person
takes orders in the office for a sandwich delivery business
his wife runs, and of course a lot of the letters written in the
firm's time are by people sorting out their bank accounts
and so on. Amazing!'

'My firm seems to specialize in long tea breaks', replies
Tom, 'I wouldn't call that work either.'

'When you work at home', Erica reflects, 'you can do
things how you want to, and don't get told "that's not the
way we do things here". Firms seem to set a lot of store by
imposing a sort of culture on you – I think it's more about
making people belong or conform, rather than about the
best way of doing the work.'

Tom says: 'You can also wear what you like at home,
can't you Erica. No great wardrobe of power-dressing suits
– jeans will do. That must mean a saving?'

'Yes', says Erica, 'I dread the era of video-phones for that
very reason – people will be able to see me looking like a
scarecrow, and it might lose me some credibility. I'll have
to smarten up my top half at least, if that comes about.
Mind you, I have to have one or two decent outfits, even
working from home, because I must look smart on visits.'

'Well, Erica', says Tom, 'you've only got another month
or so to go, so you'll soon be working back at home.'

'It can't come too soon for me', says Erica.

6

Telework and employment status

The employment status of teleworkers has some important implications both for organizations and the individual workers concerned. Teleworkers can be hired as:

- self-employed sub-contractors,
- nominally self-employed sub-contractors,
- direct employees.

Self-employed subcontractors

An organization may contract with a self-employed individual or firm of teleworkers for consultancy or freelance work. This could take the form of a short-term contract, retainer or payment by results. The workers involved are otherwise free to contract themselves out to other clients.

Nominally self-employed subcontractors

Here the teleworker would be self-employed for tax and National Insurance purposes, but does in fact rely on one single organization for the supply of work, and is thus not free to take on other clients, unlike the truly self-employed. These are sometimes known as 'quasi-employees' and this is generally recognized as a 'grey area' of employment status.

Direct employees

This occurs where a teleworker is employed on a contract

of service, whether full or part-time, short or of indeterminate duration.

The first two categories above offer relative flexibility in the amount and duration of the labour purchased. They offer advantages in terms of savings on National Insurance, PAYE and related employee benefit costs, plus the avoidance of most employment law provisions. The ease with which the arrangement can be terminated, and the fact that the risks of fluctuating demand are borne by the individual teleworker, may be seen as advantages to the utilizing organization.

There are also certain attractions to the individual of being truly self-employed. These include the fact that any income or profit from the business is taxed on the previous year's outcome, whereas Pay As You Earn (PAYE) is subject to tax at the time of payment. There are also business expenses that can be claimed if the teleworker can demonstrate that he or she is truly self-employed.

Among the disadvantages of self-employment to the individual are the associated administration costs: the need to keep records of income, expenditure, overheads such as travel and stationery, telecommunications costs and so on. There are no paid holidays or sick pay and the responsibility for pension arrangements falls on the individual.

The disadvantages to the client/contractor are that the loyalty of such staff cannot be guaranteed and, if security of information is important, this could be an issue for the employer. Turnover rates tend to be higher than with directly employed staff and, if conformity to a particular organization culture is valued, it is generally easier to engender this with direct employees.

There also evidence that, in the case of 'quasi-employees', the Inland Revenue will keep a very close eye on how the relationship operates. If they decide that a worker in actual fact has employment status, the employer may be liable to back-payment of National Insurance and PAYE contributions. If a teleworker is doubtful about the situation he or she can seek an opinion from a liaison officer in every local tax office who can make a ruling covering the Inland Revenue and DSS.

The test which is applied is whether there is a contract *of* service (employment) or a contract for services (self-employment). The Inland Revenue will apply the following indicators when assessing which category a worker falls into:

- whether there is a written contract for services, and if it can be shown that such a contract has *in fact* been followed,
- if the teleworker has control over how the service is to be provided, in what way, when and where,
- if the teleworker operates from his/her own premises, or if working at the customer's premises; whether it is clear that the teleworker is *not* subject to staff regulations, set hours of work and holidays,
- whether the teleworker can use deputies to perform the job, and whether he/she can provide services freely to several parties at the same time,
- who provides the equipment and pays for its upkeep,
- if the teleworker assumes the risk of losses, provides capital and pays insurance premiums,
- if payments are made calculated by reference to the service provided, and if invoices are issued,
- if it is clear that the teleworker has no entitlement to holiday or sick pay,
- whether the customer/employer is obliged to provide the teleworker with further work in the future,
- whether the teleworker is really free to provide services to other parties without restriction. A range of customers/clients would indicate a contract for services.

Case studies of telework schemes and American research by Olson (1981), shows that there are two emerging broad types of organization within which teleworkers operate:

- the contract organization
- the human resource organization

The contract organization

This way of organizing a distributed firm involves a pre-
dominance of 'contract' or self-employed staff. Usually
there is a 'core' of directly-employed people, by prefer-
ence, and to satisfy legal requirements. Around this core,
there are numbers of self-employed (or nominally self-
employed) workers, who provide a workforce which can
be rapidly varied to take account of fluctuations in demand
for the services of the firm, and to deploy different skills
and experience as required. Some of the objectives of such
organizations are:

- to cut costs by transforming fixed into variable costs,
- to vary staffing levels to reflect changes in demand,
- to deploy various skills where demand for them is intermittent.

The disadvantages of the contract approach are:

- there may be less commitment by contract workers to
  the firm,
- control over staff tends to be exercised by means of
  extrinsic rewards only,
- it is more difficult to ensure that behaviour conforms
  with the corporate image,
- work is often irregular which means it is up to the
  individual to ensure a regular income-flow,
- it may restrict the type of work done remotely because
  of fears about security of information.

Example of a contract organization

Chamberlain's, a distributed personnel services consultancy firm, is a spin-off from the Rank Xerox networking scheme, and is the largest enterprise that it created. The company has several different categories of staff:

- *directly employed group*: This consists of professional consultants and clerical support staff on-site, plus home-based support staff.
- *directly-employed 'permanent-temporaries'*: About 75 staff work on programming, administrative and secretarial duties at clients' premises on short-term contracts of service.
- *self-employed licensees*: There are staff working on a basis similar to franchisees, using the Chamberlain's logo and style and giving a share of the profits to the firm.
- *self-employed associates*: These are specialist freelance consultants who may be called upon to provide particular skills needed from time to time. Out of about 150, about 15 are working for Chamberlain's at any particular time.

[Source: ILO, 1990]

The human resource organization

The second type of teleworked organization is one where remote work tends to be offered to its existing employees as a way to retain their services on a directly employed basis. Teleworkers remain full corporate members of the firm and are part of the internal labour market of the organization.

Some of the objectives of such organizations are:

- to attract and retain scarce-skilled employees,

- to offer continuity of employment to women after maternity leave,
- to develop and train staff and treat them as long-term assets,
- to foster high commitment among staff.

The disadvantages of the human resource approach are:

- it offers less opportunity to respond rapidly to fluctuations in demand for the product or service,
- it is not always a cost-cutting option.

Example of a human resource organization

Hampshire County Council introduced teleworking, along with other flexible working-arrangements such as job-sharing, annual hours contracts and career-break schemes, in an effort to solve recruitment and retention problems. It is considered that round 500 posts have some scope for remote working, and the Council has begun with 20 pilot teleworkers.

In general, teleworkers will be employees, and will have the same pay and rights to sick benefit, holidays, maternity leave, pensions and other benefits enjoyed by conventional on-site employees. Pilot teleworkers include:

- a member of the social services department using a terminal connected to the Health Service network, Healthnet.
- a manager in the computer services department teleworking whilst temporarily disabled.
- a clerical support worker in the architect's department, teleworking from home following maternity leave, gradually building up hours worked.
- staff with mobility problems after long-term sick leave.

[Source: *Industrial Relations Review and Report* 1988]

7

Providing a home workstation

Setting-up costs

If your teleworkers are going to be homebased, or operate partly from home and partly at the office, you may need to provide them with a home workstation. The costs of doing this have been variously estimated at between £3000 (*DTI Remote Work Project*, 1986) and £5000 (*Industrial Relations Review and Report*, 1988). The general consensus is that the cost of computer hardware has been declining rapidly in recent years. It is as well to remember though that costs can vary quite considerably, depending upon the needs of the individual teleworker. Some will need only very simple equipment to enable them to operate successfully. Others will need a complete 'home office' with a personal computer, data transmission links, fax, printing and photocopying facilities. However, many employers will be able to utilize existing hardware items.

It is best to be guided by a clear-eyed assessment of what the individual's needs really are, rather than by someone who is 'in love' with computer equipment! Teleworkers needs may change over time as the job evolves, or as new facilities become available, so that employers will need to update home workstations just as they do 'on-site' offices.

Most organizations considering telework will have enough internal computer expertise to enable them to choose their own equipment and provide support: other firms may wish to consult bodies such as the National Computing Centre (NCC) or the Federation of Microsystems Centres, which have local offices in most parts of the country. These offer free, impartial advice on setting up a system and organizing training.

The costs of a home workstation may seem high, if one

individual working at home has exclusive use of the machinery. It may be more cost-effective to use business services local to the homeworker, if they are available, to provide photocopying or fax facilities if they are very rarely used. However, rural teleworkers may not have such facilities available nearby, and many teleworkers complain that they are denied adequate access to such services, so serious consideration should be given to providing a complete range of equipment.

Running costs

It is vital to fully quantify communications running costs before implementing work at home because, unlike setting-up costs, they are constantly recurring. All telecommunications links are costed by distance and duration rather than volume, and this can mean that a telework scheme with high 'on-line' costs may be very costly outside the local call-charge area. It is always worth considering the relative cost and efficiency of transporting data by post, fax or disk rather than via data communications links to and from the central office. Some types of teleworker, such as professionals, managers and technical employees, would make only limited use of data transmission facilities: others, such as clerical support workers might be 'on-line' for most of the working-day, and this must be taken into account when costing any scheme.

Equipment

The main hardware items are:

- telephone line, plus added services in a digital (ISDN) exchange area
- personal computer
- modem link with second telephone line

- electronic mail
- printer
- fax machine
- answering machine
- photocopier
- pager/cellphone
- laptop/handheld computer

Tables 1, 2 and 3 contain estimated costs of various items of equipment, and telephone services, for an individual home workstation, at mid-1991 prices. They illustrate the wide range of price and facilities available. The 'Basic' column represents a sensible purchase, not necessarily the cheapest. The 'Top of range' column represents the best purchases for non-specialist work.

The tables are based on average prices for single items. Bulk purchasers may be able to negotiate on price. It is always possible to buy more cheaply, or second-hand, but this can be a false saving if faults arise, or you need to return or repair. Cheaper items also sometimes have little or no potential to upgrade.

Table 1: *Computer equipment*

Basic		Top of range	
MACHINE	£800	MACHINE	£2000
286 machine VGA mono 1 Mb memory 20 Mb hard disc 1 floppy drive		386 SX SVGA colour 4 Mb memory 100 Mb hard disc dual floppy	
PRINTER	£500	PRINTER	£2000
good dot matrix or inkjet		laser with postscript dual bins	
SOFTWARE	£100	SOFTWARE	£2000
integrated package		wp package spreadsheet database desk-top publishing	
TOTAL	£1400	TOTAL	£6000

Table 2: *Some additional items*

Equipment	Basic	Top of range
MODEM[a]	£300	£600
FAX MACHINE	£450	£3000
PAGER[b]	£33	£120
CELLPHONE[c]	£350	£800
ANSWERING MACHINE	£65	£150
PORTABLE COMPUTER	£400	£5000

Table 3: *Telephone services (prices rounded)*

Installation	£152
One Year's Rental	£69
Star Services – Digital Exchange Areas[d]	
Call Diversion – One Year's Rental	£28
Three-Way Calls – One Year's Rental	£16
Call-Barring – One Year's Rental	£28

[a] modems need reasonable speed and error-checking facility to keep telephone costs down.
[b] Excludes service charge.
[c] Excludes installation and system connexion charges.
[d] There would also be charges when these services are utilized.

Problems

Many existing telework schemes have initially encountered technical problems. The most common are:

- difficulties of compatibility between systems within a scheme,
- low speed of data transmission using analogue equipment,
- difficulties with software adaptation.

The second problem should improve as the telecommunications system is upgraded: currently about half of the telephone exchanges in the UK have been converted to digital working. It would be unwise not to anticipate teething problems with any new system, which should be rectified at the pilot stage.

Who pays?

Self-employed teleworkers have to buy their own equipment, pay running costs and maintenance charges. The client firm in this case, might provide interest-free loans for subcontractors to buy their equipment. Direct employees would usually be provided with equipment, and would receive allowances towards running costs (such as rental and call charges) and overheads. The equipment would revert to the employer in the case of a person leaving or transferring back to an on-site job. The details of agreements on this should be included in a policy document or guide provided to participants.

Furniture

Besides the hardware items, other initial costs are involved in setting-up a home workstation. Employers such as Rank Xerox, Digital, and Lombard North Central will arrange for a second telephone line to be installed if necessary. Furniture for the home workstation is also usually provided, but it may be unwise for an employer to assume that furniture from existing offices can be used in the home workstation. Very often, the space available in the home is very limited, so that employers should be prepared to provide suitable-sized desks, storage equipment and so on, tailored to the needs of the individual.

The start-up costs of setting up a home workstation may appear high, but this is because they are more visible and quantifiable in the case of teleworkers. When analysing the costs and benefits of remote work, it must be borne in mind that a workstation would have to be provided if the

individual were employed on-site, as well as a separate
office in some cases, plus many other facilities such as
toilets, canteens and so on.

The ideal work area

Some employers of teleworkers specify that the workspace
should be in a separate room, others only that the equipment should be only used by the teleworker and be safe
from interference from other family members, or not in a
'family room'. There are examples of very much less than
ideal circumstances: for example a workstation based in a
domestic utility room, which became out of bounds if the
laundry was being done. Others use the dining-room table
which means work is disrupted at mealtimes. Even the
ubiquitous spare bedroom may be unavailable when relatives come to stay.

There is already a growing 'niche market' for houses
with an extra reception room or bedroom convertible into
a home office. However, this market is only available to the
more affluent teleworker: most people may have to make
the best of less than ideal circumstances.

Lombard North Central specify that the work area should:

● be quiet and undisturbed at the times work is undertaken,
● have sufficient space to set up any equipment needed:
  at least 20 square feet,
● have sufficient drawer and shelf-space to safely store
  consumables, documentation and computer disks,
● have 4 × 13 amp. power-point within 5 feet, or the
  facility to safely route an extension lead to the position,
● have a telephone point in the vicinity, or the facility to
  safely use a telephone extension lead to the position.

EC legislation

By the end of 1992, there will be minimum standards throughout the EC regarding workstations provided by employers, applying to workers who use display screens during a significant part of their working day.

Minimum standards do not just apply to the display screen itself, but also to the keyboard, work desk or work surface, work chair, software, and the general environment of the workstation itself, including space, lighting, reflection and glare, noise, heat, radiation and humidity. These requirements will not apply to mobile computer systems, or portable systems, or those mainly for public use, but would certainly apply to workstations provided by employers for home use by teleworkers.

8

Implementing a telework scheme

If a logical, planned approach to implementing a telework scheme is adopted, there is a greater chance of success than is likely to result from an ad hoc reaction based on the latest managerial fashion or fad. Even small companies with limited resources can analyse a problem, put forward alternative solutions, test them out and continually review and modify the initiative in the light of experience.

There are five stages in the planned approach:

1. identifying the problem,
2. analysis and assessment,
3. testing and developing,
4. implementation,
5. review and modification.

(see also Figure 5)

Identifying the problem

This means investigating the present state of the organization. Problems need to be identified, and if possible quantified. They may include recruitment, induction and training costs for particular occupational groupings; current retention rates; costings for accommodation and office overheads; plus possible attitude surveys of staff and their supervisors.

Analysis and assessment

The choices available to the organization should be investigated, the various options discussed and matched to the

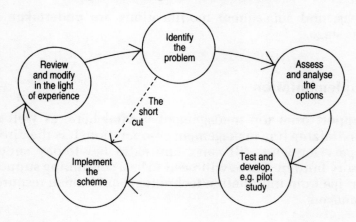

(*Source:* Adapted from NEDO/TA, 1989.)

Figure 5: *The planned approach*

expertise available within the organization. This could be undertaken by an individual or, in a larger firm, by a working group with a mix of specialist skills, usually including information technology and human resources. At this stage it may be decided to use outside consultants if the internal knowledge is felt to need supplementing and if the organization can afford it.

Line managers and trade union representatives should be involved if appropriate. Through using project groups, firms may discover local initiatives or schemes which could be of value.

Testing and developing

Telework schemes, particularly those which involve work at home, are usually tested by limited pilot schemes over a six-month period, designed to demonstrate their practicality and acceptability to staff. The identification of problem areas, and subsequent modifications are undertaken at this stage.

Implementation

Support from top management is vital here, as well as maximizing line management co-operation. It is the direct supervisor who will carry any extra day-to-day supervisory burden. There will need to be a continuing support service from information technology and human resource managers.

Review and modification

Unexpected problems and consequences are bound to arise from any new working pattern, and these may affect on-site staff as well as teleworkers and their supervisors. For example, elements of the benefits package offered to teleworkers may cause resentment among on-site staff, and this might lead to modifications in the fringe benefits offered to all types of staff.

Best practice

The best telework schemes tend to have the following characteristics:

- Even where schemes are very limited in scope, the effects on the whole organization are considered prior to implementation and the human resource strategy linked to overall business strategy.
- Top executives back the scheme and are involved in its development.
- Human resource, IT and line managers (and trade

unions where recognized) work as a team to develop the initiative.

- The potential teleworkers (if internal recruits are used) are involved at an early stage, and are at the centre of the piloting and implementation process.
- The objections and anxieties of the potential teleworkers, colleagues and supervisors are not dismissed as unimportant but used as systems design criteria.
- Training is given to suit individual needs before implementation.
- Teleworker feedback after implementation is used positively to improve the scheme.

Questions which should be asked

There are a number of questions which should be addressed at each of the planning stages. The following list is a general guide: each organization's particular situation will also throw up its own unique problems and challenges.

At the problem stage

- what precisely is our problem?
- how can the problem be quantified?
- how does our problem compare with other local firms, those in the same sector or region as a whole?

At the analysis stage

- why choose telework rather than other options?
- will telework fit in with organizational objectives and culture?
- how much expertise do we have in human resources and IT?
- do we need to bring in consultants?
- which jobs should we consider for telework?
- do they require modification?

- should we do an attitude survey of potential teleworkers and supervisors?
- which work-pattern is most suitable?
- what equipment is needed?
- how much will running costs be?
- how will teleworkers be supervised?
- will recruits be internal or external?
- what are the legal, health and safety, tax and insurance implications?
- what type of employment contract will we operate?
- what will be the effects on other groups in the organization?
- where shall we locate a satellite office?
- what are the labour market trends in the chosen location(s)?
- what are the telecommunications facilities like there?
- Is the local authority and Chamber of Commerce in the satellite location favourable to our scheme?
- what suitable accommodation is available?
- what are the fixed costs?
- what are transport links like to Head Office?
- can we 'sell' this location to the top decision makers?

If internal recruits are used

- how will the potential teleworkers participate in the scheme?
- what happens if some are willing (to become home-based, for example) and others are not?
- will some of the group remain on-site?
- what training will they need?
- what support will line managers need?
- should pilot teleworkers be seasoned employees or new recruits?
- what about appraisal, development and discipline?

If external recruits are used

- is there a sufficient labour supply of the quality we need where we need it?
- how will they be inducted, trained and developed?
- what type of employment contract will they be offered?
- what pay, fringe benefits and allowances will they be offered?
- what should be included in the job description and employee specification?
- what recruitment channels should be used to access a particular group?

At the testing stage

- what problems have arisen during the pilot?
- can the project be successfully modified?
- has the pilot achieved the original objectives?
- should we implement a wider-scale project, or not?

At the implementation stage

- how can we successfully involve all the parties in implementation?
- what are the training needs?
- how can we ensure continual feedback and modification?
- what continued support do we need to offer to line managers?
- shall we formally review the scheme after an interval?

9

Job analysis, recruitment and selection

Job analysis

IT World consultants (1991) specializing in developing telework schemes estimate that 10 per cent of jobs are suitable for telework, and a further 15 per cent could be made suitable if modifications were made to how the tasks within a job were carried out. They advocate that managers should be more innovative and questioning when analysing jobs.

An analysis of each job being considered for telework should be carried out in order to ascertain whether it can be modified to accommodate some form of remote working. Job analysis is the process of collecting information from various sources about the tasks, responsibilities and context of a job. Once a job analysis has been undertaken, it can form the basis for a job description and a person specification which can be used for recruitment and selection purposes. The information is also useful as a basis for assessing job performance and for ascertaining training needs.

The information which makes up a job analysis should include:

- *job title, division, department, etc,*
- *relationships with others*: reporting, supervisory, liaison, co-ordination,
- *job content*: tasks and duties, important and intermittent tasks.
- *working conditions*: physical and social environment, times of work, salary and benefits.
- *performance standards*: these can be quantitative and qualitative, for example, amount of sales volume and/or the quality of relationships with clients or customers.

- *human requirements*: physical or psychological characteristics of the person fitted to do the job.

The transformation of a job to teleworking mode may change the nature of several aspects of a job previously performed on-site.

Relationships with others

The network of relationships of an on-site job-incumbent will inevitably be changed or restricted by a move to remote work. The incumbent, supervisor and other people involved with the job could construct a 'role-set' diagram for the on-site job. This involves charting the key people and groups with whom the job-holder has to work.

The chart needs to indicate:

- the *volume* of contact needed with each group or individual,
- the most *influential* role-set members.

David Rees, in his book *The Skills of Management* (1991), advocates that a diagram should indicate influence by the proximity to the person in the centre, and indicate frequency by the size of the circle around a person or group. This is illustrated in Figure 6, which shows the role-set of a bank employee.

Once a role-set diagram has been agreed, it can form a basis for discussion on how communication can be modified or 'batched', to allow remote work, what communication can be done by computer or telephone and what face-to-face interaction is necessary. Informal contact with peers should not be overlooked, because though it may not be considered important on a daily basis, it may be vital as a channel for exchanging views, experiences and strategies for solving job-related problems.

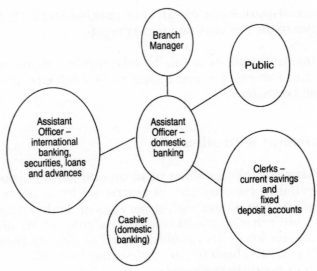

(*Source:* from Rees, D., *The Skills of Management*, 1991.)

Figure 6: *Role-set diagram*

Job content

An analysis of the main tasks within a job is vital in order to ascertain whether the job is suitable for telework, or can be adapted to accommodate it. There must be a considerable element of individual working, and a reasonable period of time between deadlines but, against that, no great areas of uncharted time. If a teleworker is to undertake project work, if it is long term, it may be advisable to break it down into segments so that progress can be regularly monitored.

Some jobs can be considered for telework only by excluding certain tasks, which would have to be carried out on-site, or where security of information is required. However, with sophisticated computer equipment and the use of entry codes, the issue of security of data can be addressed. Paradoxically, it is probably more difficult to ensure security if sensitive *written* documents have to be taken home.

Working conditions

Telework, particularly the work-at-home variety, will have profound effects on the lifestyle of incumbents, particularly where previously they have worked in an office environment. The physical environment must be considered, including heat, noise, lighting, health and safety implications as well as legal, tax and insurance consequences (see Chapters 14 and 15). Time of work will also be an issue: whether complete autonomy will be given to teleworkers, or if there is to be a duty to work certain hours. Also, whether or not there is opportunity for any work in teams should be included. Salary and benefits may also be affected by the change in work-pattern: consideration should be given to special allowances, for heating, lighting and telecommunications costs for home-based teleworkers (see Chapter 10).

Performance standards and objectives

Both quantitative and qualitative standards of work will remain important for teleworkers, but may be more difficult to monitor at a distance, particularly the qualitative variety. Methods of supervision are discussed in more detail in Chapter 11.

Human requirements

A lot of stress is laid in the literature on particular psychological attributes being needed by teleworkers. Some feel that teleworkers must have low affiliation needs, be 'self-starters' and be able to cope with isolation. We feel that too much stress has been laid on these traits, and social factors are rather more important than psychological ones. We believe that a positive motivation towards telework, or a pressing need to be home-based, and having a suitable remote working environment, is probably more important than a particular psychological make-up. Most telework jobs – and certainly those in the professional, technical and managerial field – will need good interpersonal skills, and an ability to get on with people, whether meeting face-to-face or over the telephone. This would tend to preclude people with a tendency to introversion.

If the human requirements for telework are too specific and restrictive, managers may find few people qualified to perform the job. Also the potential of people may be overlooked. Many of the attributes useful to teleworkers, like good time-management or negotiating skills, can be learned, so that if training is made available, this will widen the pool of potential internal or external recruits.

Recruitment and selection

Recruits for telework may be existing employees, or they may be sought on the external labour market. Another source of potential teleworkers is former employees who may have relevant skills and previous on-site experience with a firm.

Internal recruits

If teleworkers are recruited from among the existing workforce, they should *always* be volunteers, and the effects on their careers and benefits carefully considered and discussed with the individual or group concerned. There may be legal implications of a change of work pattern which should be borne in mind, such as contractual law and anti-discrimination legislation.

A number of the pilot studies have only used self-selecting 'seasoned employees' as teleworkers, often with several years service with the firm, so that they are a known quantity and their previous work performance and attributes are satisfactory. There are examples, however, where the decision has been taken to transform entire occupational groupings into home-based workers, and this will mean that quite new recruits will become remote workers, and in the future, recruits to that work category will be external.

External recruits

If it is decided to recruit from the external labour market, it must be borne in mind that they may come from a more dispersed geographical area, and this may affect the choice of recruitment media. Other groups may be more difficult to access, and some thought about suitable recruitment media may be necessary. These groups can include the disabled, early retired, carers, women with young families and people with specific IT skills. Whichever is chosen, the recruitment method must be fair to all potential applicants, and should not, in its effect, deter minorities or members of one sex from applying.

Flexible working hours and location, clearly specified, can be used as a feature to attract staff. Advertising should make clear what on-site attendance is necessary, and whether visits to clients' premises are also involved. The employment status and the duration of the contract should also be made clear to potential recruits. In some cases, employers use a short-term contract as a probationary device for teleworkers, and this should be clearly stated.

When employers are organizing the time and place for interviews, the constraints on the potential recruits should be borne in mind. Some flexibility may be necessary on the part of the employer to ensure that people are able to attend.

Choosing a teleworker on a contract-for-service basis brings into play somewhat different skills of tendering, negotiating and assessing the reputation of the individual or firm. This can be done through a professional association, or by recommendation from other companies who have used consultants or subcontractors for similar areas of work.

Some teleworked organizations use psychological testing as part of the selection process, particularly to assess the ability to cope with social isolation. Psychological tests should be administered and interpreted by properly trained staff, and should not be the sole criterion for selection, but only one part of the selection process.

10

Pay, conditions and allowances

When telework is contemplated, like any other new work-ing pattern, the issue of pay and benefits must be consi-dered carefully. The nature of pay will be related to the type of contract which teleworkers are given. If, for ex-ample, they are self-employed, then no fringe benefits can be given as this will undermine the self-employed status of the teleworker.

Employers should take into account existing legislation on equal pay and discrimination to ensure that their pay and benefits package does not break the law. For example, deciding to pay female homeworkers less than equivalent male workers on-site may contravene the law. Also it is important to consider whether teleworkers will be paid on occasions if no work can be provided for them and during periods of sickness or absence.

Pay

As we saw in Chapter 3, telework as a pattern of work can involve many types of job category, and the chosen pay-ment system of home-based workers may be very variable and reflect the tradition of equivalent on-site work. Mana-gers and professionals, for example, are likely to be paid a monthly salary, whereas clerical staff may receive a weekly wage. However, with its emphasis on 'output mode', telework would seem logically to be suited to some form of payment by results. In other cases, the payment method appears to reflect the traditions of the type of work involved, rather than the contingencies of the situation. For example, software programmers at FI and ICL who work remotely are usually paid on a time basis, with homeworkers filling in time-sheets.

Self-employed teleworkers are retained, paid a fee, or paid by output (word-processing for example). The pay and tax implications for those who are nominally self-employed subcontractors may need some clarification, and this is available from the DSS or Inland Revenue (see Chapter 6).

An employer may decide to use a payment system for teleworkers which differs from that operating for on-site employees, particularly by way of directly linking pay to output. The implications of the change must be carefully considered. Another factor which must be discussed is the question of overtime. If telework implies that working hours are flexible then the concept of overtime working is unlikely to apply. Again, equity and fairness between the treatment of on-site and distance workers must be considered.

Patricia Leighton and Michael Syrett, in their 1989 book, *New Work Patterns: Putting Policy Into Practice*, feel that performance-related pay could be adapted to cover many types of remote worker, on the basis of a minimum number of hours worked, or length of service. Pay related to the performance of the enterprise, such as share option schemes or profit-related pay, are usually restricted to long-serving permanent staff, and must be approved by the Inland Revenue. There is some evidence that part-timers are sometimes included in such schemes, but usually only after a qualifying period of employment.

Benefits

As far as fringe benefits are concerned, many 'perks' valued by on-site employees are not suitable for remote workers, particularly totally home-based staff. Examples include car allowances, subsidized canteens and assistance with travel. These workers may prefer to have assistance with childcare costs, or financial incentives. Some companies are developing a system of 'cafeteria' benefits from which employees can choose. Though more expensive to run, this system would offer flexibility to match employees' particular situations.

Other benefits may be considered as desirable for both on-site staff and teleworkers. These include access to occupational pension schemes, sick pay and holiday entitlement. For part-time teleworkers these could be offered on a pro rata basis.

Childcare

One of the groups which employers often wish to recruit, or to retain, using home-based telework is women with young children, and this work pattern is one way of bridging the career gap for women. It would, however, be a mistake to assume that because this group would often work totally, or predominantly at home, that their childcare problems have been automatically solved. FI software programmers, over 90 per cent of whom are women with young families, must arrange for childcare, and cannot work only in the periods when their children are asleep. Childcare problems do not disappear once children are of school-age – in fact it could be argued that the situation often becomes more complicated – there are long holidays, half-terms and odd days off. A lack of assistance with childcare costs is consistently cited as a major disadvantage of this form of work in surveys of women teleworkers. Many do continue to fit work around domestic commitments, by working early in the morning or late at night. It would be worthwhile for employers to consider providing some financial assistance with childcare, in order to increase the effectiveness and productivity of this group of workers and reduce stress levels.

Except in satellite offices, remote workers could not take advantage of workplace nurseries, but there are alternatives. Employers could offer a childcare allowance, or childcare vouchers, and/or offer help in finding suitable childminders. If an allowance were given, this would give the teleworker an element of choice as to how to spend the money, which would vary with the particular job and family circumstances. They may choose to put it towards the cost of a nursery place, domestic nanny or childminder, or to pay for holiday or after-school supervision for their older children.

Allowances

There are very different approaches to providing allowances to teleworkers for items like extra heating, electricity and telecommunications costs. Some employers calculate that the extra costs of working at home are balanced by savings on travel and clothing costs, and therefore offer no extra allowances. Training Standards Inspectors teleworking for the Training Agency, (1989) considered that the savings did not compensate for the additional expenditure and pressed for a home-based worker allowance. This was being discussed with the Treasury.

Other employers have a well worked-out allowance system. Lombard North Central's teleworkers on a pilot scheme can claim part of the cost of telephone rental, business phone calls, a domestic power allowance, postage allowance and costs of essential business travel. Digital (DEC Ltd) pay an annual allowance to teleworkers to cover heat, light and inconvenience which is reviewed every year.

We would advocate the approach adopted by Lombard North Central and Digital because it avoids resentment among teleworkers that they are being treated unfairly, and will tend to increase the loyalty of remote staff towards the organization.

All allowances which an employer is planning to pay to teleworkers should be discussed with the Inland Revenue before a scheme is implemented, to ascertain the income tax position of employees.

Allowances could include:

- a flat-rate allowance towards home energy costs,
- allowance for household wear and tear,
- payment of the costs of installing a second telephone line,
- payment of telephone rental costs,
- payment for business telephone calls and data transmission costs,
- travel allowance for itinerant staff,
- postal allowance for business use.

11

Communications, control and supervision

Difficulties with communication are often cited by managers with no direct experience of telework as the most important reason for rejecting a move to telework. But Huws, Korte and Robinson's survey (1990) found that it is a fairly minor problem for managers actually employing teleworkers.

Because social isolation is often mentioned by remote workers as a disadvantage of this type of work-arrangement, the object of good communications is to avoid excluding teleworkers from aspects of on-site work, such as internal telephone directories, house journals, outings, competitions, social gatherings, internally advertised job opportunities, as well as literature from trade unions or associations which represent staff. Communications between teleworkers should be encouraged and opportunities provided to meet face to face, both for work and social purposes.

Teamwork

If the type of work permits, teleworkers should be given the opportunity to work as part of a team or project group. Software programmers often work in this way, as can fieldworkers or inspectors. Training Standards Inspectors working for the Training Agency also have opportunities to work on joint inspections, which lead to a cross-fertilization of ideas, and assist in the personal development of the remote workers.

For those with little job experience, or where knowledge of unusual or hazardous situations needs to be shared, regular contact with colleagues is very important in performing the job. Supervisors are likely to have to devote more time to junior staff, whereas more experienced individuals will probably need little supervision.

There are many types of dispersed organizations – franchised operations for example – which have to expend more energy and time on communications because of the way they are organized, but it is not seen as an insurmountable problem. However, it is a new problem for many managers who have become used to using direct communication methods in an office setting.

Communication methods

Some of the communication methods which can be used are:

- electronic mail,
- allocating a 'mentor' to each teleworker,
- face to face get-togethers,
- development and training meetings,
- social occasions,
- regular managerial visits to teleworkers,
- neighbourhood centres.

Control and supervision

Teleworking involves control and supervision at a distance, and this presents line managers with new challenges. According to Paul Jackson, a researcher at Cambridge University, there are three main ways of controlling and supervising teleworkers:

- control by the market,
- control by electronics,
- control by formal reporting systems.

Control by the market

Where a teleworker is self-employed, financial control is effected by the 'going-rate' for the job, payment by results, or payment by deliverables or segments of work. This would apply both to the professional and consultancy sector of the market, where individuals would be retained or paid a fee, as well as to clerical support functions, such as data input or wordprocessing, where they would be paid for output. Quality of results and performance, as well as quantity of work, would also have to be taken into account.

Control by electronics

IT equipment itself can be used to monitor output and productivity. This can take various forms, giving different levels of autonomy and independence. Sales representatives and mobile insurance staff usually give daily feedback on results via their mobile or personal computers: data input workers can be measured much more closely, by the 'bytes' of information processed and error rates. The equipment can also be used to monitor remote telesales or directory staff by recording the time taken to respond to the telephone, or the number of enquiries dealt with in a period of time. Where segments of work are 'queued' by the computer, such as insurance claims, similar control systems can be utilized.

Systems are currently being developed whereby remote workers can request rest periods through the electronics system and will have their time at work and rate of work continually monitored, and compared to the average for other similar workers. The recent EC Directive on health and safety for VDU users (90/270/EEC) which will be translated into British law by the end of 1992, states that systems *must* provide feedback to workers on their performance, and that no quantitative or qualitative checking facility may be used without the worker's knowledge.

The very close supervision methods (almost a throw-back to the kind of 'scientific management' F. W. Taylor proposed in his famous 1911 book of that name) which such workers work under on-site will probably be replicated at a distance through information technology. In the case of many back-office workers, there will be no increase in autonomy or independence through work-at-home – it will be a much more socially isolated and impersonal version of on-site working conditions.

Surveys of existing teleworkers show that relatively few are in fact monitored in this way. The main reason for this is that there are, as yet, relatively few teleworkers undertaking back-office functions. Consistently this group is underrepresented in telework surveys. They may be the teleworkers of tomorrow.

Control by formal reporting systems

This type of control is used for managerial, technical and professional staff, field-workers and IT professionals. The supervisor and teleworker jointly decide on tasks and objectives, and, if necessary, methods to be used. The teleworker is then left to work relatively unsupervised until the next formal interaction. This appears to be the most common type of control at the moment. The supervisor becomes a co-ordinator or orchestrator, rather than being intimately involved in how a task is performed. Some existing schemes, particularly for software programmers, have very close monitoring systems, with work split into short time-segments. This may reflect the unique nature of each project, and the need to prevent cost over-runs, but Huws, Korte and Robinson (1990) feel that it may be due to individual company style or culture. Such close control may not necessarily be needed with other types of work, or in an organization with a different culture.

The manager's role

The issue of control and supervision of teleworkers is perhaps the most important perceived barrier to the wider diffusion of telework. Many managers are fearful of change and disruption to the traditional patterns of organizing work. In particular managers' lack of trust in their staff, even where they are highly qualified and experienced, seems to be a great problem, which has led in some cases to over-elaborate, expensive monitoring systems leading to resentment among teleworkers, in others to very formal, impersonal communications.

The positive motivation of telework supervisors and managers is crucial to the success of any scheme for corporate remote workers; they may need to be trained for new skills of remote management, preferably before new working patterns are introduced. Besides setting and monitoring task objectives, managers may have to act as a vital link between homeworkers, as well as a bridge between them and the mainstream organization.

Case study: managing teleworkers

The Line-Manager's Tale

Jeff Sommerby is a manager in a medium-sized company in the financial services sector. He has been closely involved in the implementation of a pilot teleworking scheme and supervises teleworkers as well as office-based staff undertaking computer software design and development work. He feels that the time and hard work involved in the changes have been well-worthwhile:

> The human aspect of telework is just as important – more really – than the technical side. It's a different style of management in effect – you may need to give people more support, at least initially, and it's a discipline for you as well – it can show up a manager's weaknesses in fact.

There were some initial doubts among line managers here – myself included – about what supervising teleworkers would mean. The main anxieties were that supervising home-based people would take up a lot more of our time and overload us. Also some felt they might lose control of their staff. (That hasn't happened, by the way.) Security of data was another thing – we've overcome that through the technology, passwords and so on.

The people I supervise have quite a lot of contact with the office. Besides the usual face-to-face sort, like discussions and meetings to oversee the progress of each project, there are other modes – telephoned, faxed or electronic messages and memos, plus the old-fashioned postal system for some less urgent items. This means that our home-based people have just as much contact really as the office-based ones, it's just that the character of it has changed.

All the teleworkers I supervise have previously worked in the office here, and have obviously built up a picture of how the organization works, who to contact to solve a particular problem for example. Also, of course, they all know each other pretty well and work well together as a team. We put a lot of emphasis on team-building here: although they go off and work physically on their own, they've got that back-up there if they need it.

We also make sure the teleworkers are included in all the get-togethers and are given all the information that on-site people get. It would be easy to forget to include them because you see them less often, so you need to make a particular point of doing that.

I think if telework does take off, and we're into recruiting people from the outside straight into working remotely, we'll be into a different ball-game. They won't have that depth of knowledge of the organization – that could be a problem. In that case there would have to be a more formal system of developing contacts, and probably more initial training for new recruits. Building a team-feeling would obviously be more difficult in those circumstances, but I'm sure we could overcome that.

So far we haven't had any failures – people who aren't coming up to scratch performance-wise – but that may be because we've chosen them so carefully. If we extend the scheme, then it's bound to happen that an individual won't make the grade. But then that happens in the office from time to time, so really it won't be much different. It's the same with anything new – if one person fails then it seems to cast doubt on the whole thing. I suppose it's similar to the first woman in a firm who is promoted to top management – if she doesn't make a go of it then people generalize and assume that all women are unsuitable.

If the firm's strategy changes or something external happens that changes our pattern of development, then, yes, it's possible we won't need teleworkers any more, and we'll discontinue the project. Or maybe personnel will look at a different section of the workforce – clerical people or inspectors – for remote work. We'll continue to do it for as long as it fits in with our needs, in this case to prune office overheads and retain certain shortage skills we need. Everything in business changes very rapidly these days – and of course with the European Single Market not far off that's the thing our company has already begun to plan for.

12

Training and development

Although there are particular problems associated with training and staff development at remote locations, employers need to consider this issue if teleworkers are to become full members of the organization for which they work. Unfortunately, the tradition of 'outwork' in Britain has been closely associated with an avoidance of any commitment to training, but if 'hightech' homework is really to be seen as fundamentally different, employers need to demonstrate this primarily through their training and development planning for teleworkers.

This chapter will discuss training under the following headings:

- training media,
- induction training,
- training for the current job,
- long-term development,
- management development,
- promotion,
- appraisal.

Training media

There are a number of media commonly used by trainers in putting together training schemes for conventional, on-site staff. Where staff are partly, or wholly home-based, or field-workers, the employer will need to choose a mix of the most appropriate media for learning purposes. If tele-workers are carers or people with domestic commitments, or disabled and homebound, the most flexible remote media should be chosen to match the particular needs of individuals.

Human inputs

Teleworkers need a focal point of contact within the employing organization. He or she may be in the personnel department but, more commonly, the direct line supervisor or manager will also be the trainer. This relationship is of particular significance for remote staff and may in some cases be the only direct link between the individual and the on-site organization. It is a vital one in terms of providing encouragement and help to trainees.

Training methods

Some types of training are particularly suitable for remote workers. Computers have long been used to provide self-paced learning, where the material is devised to teach and test whether learning has taken place. Videos are also widely used, and can provide suitable material for home-use. The Open University style of training, using mixed media with trainees controlling the pace and timing of learning, could provide a model to follow providing there is always human back-up. An example of distance learning, using computers with video links, comes from the University of London. Birkbeck College has a Masters' course with 100 students currently working in this way. If possible this should be supplemented by on-site training.

On-site training

On-site training will usually include delivery methods including lectures, group discussions, case studies and role-plays, and enables teleworkers to develop and sustain peer relationships as well as learn about the back-up services available on-site. When organizing on-site meetings and lectures the location, timing and duration should be tailored to suit the constraints of the individual teleworkers. For example, women with domestic commitments may prefer on-site visits which fit in with school hours or when childcare can be most easily arranged. Disabled staff may prefer to attend at a location near to home, rather than having to undertake a longer journey.

Induction training

Where teleworkers are recruited from the external labour market, they need the same care in their introduction to the employing organization as conventional staff. Leighton and Syrett (1989) list the start-up information needed:

- general information about the organization, its activities, history, culture and geographical location.
- information about regulations covering:
  - health and safety,
  - time-keeping,
  - dress conventions (if appropriate).
- information relating to benefits and facilities open to the particular job category, which might include:
  - holiday entitlement,
  - sickness payments,
  - maternity benefits,
  - pension schemes,
  - career counselling,
  - training facilities,
  - staff discounts,
  - sports and social facilities,
  - travel allowances.
- specific information about the role of their department/ hierarchy and the key people who will support/work with them, including technical support (hardware and software), information and helplines.

Induction training for teleworkers can be seen as particularly crucial, because it is only too easy for them *not* to feel a part of the organization. The timing of this learning may also be important. For example, several of the Training Inspectors employed by the Training Agency (TA) would have preferred a tour of the Regional Office, and information about the TA and its roles and responsibilities a few months *after* starting work rather than at the initial stage. New recruits often experience information saturation or overload at the beginning. The temptation to cram in as much as possible in a short timescale may be even more compelling with remote workers, whose time on-site may be limited.

Training for the current job

If computer skills are involved in job-specific training, the computer itself can be used as a medium for training either on-site or at home. The best training is:

- Tailored to the competence level the individual has already reached rather than 'blanket' coverage.
- Given at the appropriate time, i.e. *before* implementation of a telework scheme, with time to practise skills and reach acceptable performance levels.
- Supplemented by follow-up training as the computer system evolves, and/or to learn more sophisticated computer skills.

Besides computer-related skills, and according to the precise nature of their work, remote workers may need training in:

- time-management,
- priority setting,
- office systems,
- telephone skills,
- interpersonal skills.

Interpersonal skills are particularly important for field-workers, because they will represent the company to clients and customers. Remote staff are much more cut off from the 'organizational culture' and agreed ways of doing things, so that these skills may need to be learned in a more formal way than is necessary with on-site staff. The training of sales representatives may be a useful model here.

For self-employed teleworkers, there may be an additional need to learn financial management and control skills. For this group there is ample provision through small business training courses, which are now the responsibility of local Training and Enterprise Councils (TECs), in Scotland by Local Enterprise Councils (LECs).

Long-term development

The issue of long-term career development for teleworkers is a crucial test for this work pattern. The Empirica survey of teleworkers found that their sample felt they had diminished long-term development prospects because of their lack of contact with professional colleagues. Employers need to give this issue some thought and ensure that individuals' career potential is not stunted because of remote work.

Career development for staff should include:

- communication to them of all internally advertised posts,
- access to formal training courses,
- inclusion in mailing lists for conferences, etc.,
- access to open and distance learning training courses (with some human interface),
- continuing opportunities to interact with peers and supervisors to share problems and experiences.

Management development

Despite the recent emphasis in much management literature concerning 'portable' careers and 'serial monogamy'
among managers, most of this group, including teleworking managers, will continue to be dependent upon the
internal career structure of the employing organization for
their career advancement.

Management development is particularly concerned
with developing the whole person, rather than learning
narrowly defined skills, which makes formal and informal
job experiences very important. Also, managers are
developed for their future potential as well as for the current job. This makes the development of a remote worker
into a manager much more difficult than a conventional
employee.

A disadvantage of telework is its lack of visibility and
opportunities to develop and demonstrate social skills
within the workplace. Management development is
dependent as much on *who* you know as *what* you know,
and this is certainly a barrier for workers who are home-
based and only have limited face-to-face contact with colleagues and superiors. This would be less of a problem for
teleworkers in a completely remotely based hierarchy than
for those whose colleagues mostly continue to work on-
site in a conventional manner.

Promotion

In many existing telework schemes, either there are only
limited opportunities for promotion or they have not been
in existence long enough for the issue to have become
important. Some job categories of teleworkers would
expect only limited promotion prospects, but others
would have higher expectations. A lack of promotion
opportunities is often a disincentive for corporate staff to
take up telework.

One way to overcome this is to ensure that periods spent working remotely count equally with on-site service towards promotion. To ensure that lack of visibility is minimized, employers could consider using telework very flexibly, alternating periods of remote and on-site working. Employees may be very keen to work at home in the short-term, but may not wish to be home-based for a long period of time (this is one factor which would not emerge from a six-month trial period). In other cases, it might be possible to provide promotion opportunities which enable the tele-worker to continue to work remotely.

For the self-employed teleworker, particularly the more privileged group including professionals and technical specialists, advancement is a rather different issue, being dependent upon their reputation with clients or custom-ers. This is built up through their own skill and judgement. Huws, Korte and Robinson (1990) found that remote work, for this group, was not seen as a hindrance to career development.

Appraisal

With the increasing popularity of performance-related pay, as well as the importance of career development, appraisal systems are seen as vital for almost all groups of employees. Teleworkers, if they are to be developed within the organization, need to be included within the appraisal system. However, because of their mode of work-ing, the appraisal system may need some adaptation.

The uses of appraisal are:

- to set performance objectives,
- to evaluate past performance,
- to improve current performance,
- to assess training needs,
- to assess potential,

- to decide on career planning,
- to decide salary level.

Appraisal criteria

Many existing appraisal schemes involve criteria which produce judgements about how a job or task is performed, as well as the meeting of task objectives. Behaviour rating scales or observation scales are clearly unsuitable for appraising remote workers because they involve 'over-the-shoulder' methods of assessing how well work is carried out. Appraisal for teleworkers must involve judgements of performance based on the amount and quality of output, rather than the detailed methods used to produce it.

A suitable system for this group of workers would be some form of management by objectives, or a link with job analysis whereby performance standards which are identified are compared with actual performance. This is a method particularly suitable for smaller organizations, which may not have the resources to invest in a sophisticated appraisal system.

If a management by objectives system is chosen, the targets need ideally to be mutually agreed between the parties, and designed to give the teleworker a good deal of discretion as to how the objectives are to be achieved.

A problem for supervisors might be created in a situation where a job category is split, with some staff working remotely, and others in a conventional office situation. There may need to be two parallel appraisal systems, one based on output, the other on output *and* behavioural criteria. This could lead to some resentment on the part of on-site staff, especially if appraisal is linked to salary review.

13

Flexible accommodation

The fact that work is now seen to take place not only at the office but in transit, in client's premises, and in the home, is going to have profound effects on how office space is interpreted and utilized in the future. With the growth of the 'flexi-place' workforce, space in the office itself will have to be used more adaptably.

Architects are now designing office complexes as 'office villages' with built-in shopping and recreational facilities, or as 'office clubs' containing workstations and areas for meetings and discussions. Charles Handy, for example, in his book, *The Age of Unreason* (1989), describes a design consultancy firm run from a converted warehouse. It contained no offices, just a meeting-room, large kitchen, drawing-boards, word-processors, telephones and computers. No-one had a dedicated, individual workstation, except the administrative staff. Most of the consultants' time was spent with clients or at home. They came into 'the office' for meetings, to use specialist equipment and generally to keep in touch. The 'working club' idea allows the employer to equip it more lavishly than a set of individual separate offices, but this idea only works in a business with a network of individuals who work away from the office most of the time. There would be a 'core' of people in most businesses who would continue to work predominantly conventional hours, on-site, to provide an administrative and support function, and the size of this core would vary with the contingencies of the situation of the firm.

Other organizations would continue to employ most of their staff in a conventional way, but some adaptation in the use of office space would still be desirable, in order to provide space for teleworkers to attend meetings or training sessions and use office equipment and resources, and to meet each other to discuss problems and experiences. Pat Leighton and Michael Syrett (1989) suggest a three-tier system:

1. *individual allocation*: Here offices or workstations for on-site staff would be in more or less constant use during working hours.
2. *shared allocation*: Here space would be shared by a specified number of individuals during the working week. They would combine home, office and mobile work.
3. *random allocation*: Here space would be used by tele-workers on routine visits or for meetings or training sessions. Some of this space would have to be rostered in advance.

The ratio between the three categories would vary with the balance of the particular workforce.

Even employing organizations which do not have expensive prestige workplaces could adapt their office space to suit a more 'flexi-place' workforce without a great deal of effort and expense, and in many cases employers would need less space overall, enabling savings in overhead costs to be made.

14

Health and safety

General health and safety provisions are set out principally in the Health and Safety at Work Act (1974), but domestic legislation is increasingly being supplemented by EC Directives, which will have to be adopted by member states. Most of these statutes are very general in nature, but of particular interest to telework employers are supplementary directives on display equipment (VDUs) and requirements for computer workstations. Laws apply equally to all employees and the location of their work is not specified. A problem concerning workers based partly or wholly at home, is that of ensuring a sufficient level of monitoring to ensure reasonable safety standards, without interfering with the privacy of the home. Another problem is the growing use of subcontracted staff, and how they are to be adequately informed and protected.

General obligations

Employers have a general obligation to provide a safe and healthy environment for workers and to aim for continuous improvement, reducing or eliminating risks and providing information and training to employees. The EC general directive (89/391/EEC) also mentions situations where several undertakings share a workplace, which could presumably include local centres and telecottages. It states that the employers involved should co-operate and co-ordinate their actions in terms of promoting health and safety. It also clearly states that subcontracted staff, as well as direct employees, are entitled to adequate health and safety information.

Health and safety training should be provided for employees when recruited, and subsequently as technology or work processes change. Subcontracted workers should also be aware of safe procedures. Workers themselves also have obligations to follow correct procedures and rules on health and safety. All employers are obliged to have a written health and safety policy, and this should apply and be made known to remote workers, whether employed or subcontracted.

Health checks for teleworkers

Teleworkers may be employed on an intermittent, part-time or full-time basis, and employers must decide whether health screening should apply equally to remote and on-site staff. In terms of staff making considerable use of VDU equipment, the EC directive which will be adopted in December 1992, states that workers should have an eye test:

- before starting display-screen work,
- at regular intervals after that, and
- if they experience visual difficulties.

The issue of health screening for remote staff will continue to be just as important as for those with a more conventional work pattern, and in particular for 'back-office' workers who will be making the greatest use of display equipment during their working day.

Visual display equipment (VDUs)

Until new legislation on VDUs is introduced to comply with the EC directive, guidance is available free from the Health and Safety Executive (Working with VDUs, 1990). They advocate that employers should provide ergonomically designed furniture, and a workstation which is adjustable to individual needs. The VDU should be maintained to a good standard to avoid eye-strain, and the lighting should be adequate and avoid glare. The operator should be able to take frequent, short breaks (this is also important to help prevent repetitive strain injury). The user of the system should be consulted on its design, and training in good keyboard technique and other health matters should be given.

The EC Directive on display equipment can be summed up as follows:

- it does not apply to portable computer systems, or those mainly for public use, or those on modes of transport, but would apply to home workstations.
- employers should evaluate how healthy workstations are, on-site or otherwise.
- employers should comply with minimum standards laid down for screens, keyboards, work desk or space, work chair, space, lighting, glare, noise, heat, radiation, humidity and software.
- workers should have adequate health and safety information about their workstation.
- workers should receive training before starting display unit work, and when work is modified.
- workers should take frequent, short breaks.
- workers should have eyesight tests before starting display work, and at intervals, and if they have problems.

There has also been controversy about a possible link between VDU work and miscarriages. A US government study tends to refute this. Researchers compared miscarriage rates of 2400 women, and found no difference between women working with VDUs and those who did not. Working more than 25 hours a week with a display screen made no significant difference (*Guardian*, 1991, quoting research published in the *New England Journal of Medicine*).

Monitoring safety

As with the general supervision of teleworkers, the problem with health and safety provisions is how to ensure
these are followed by remote staff. Unless they are monitored for work-breaks by the equipment, there is really no
sure way of knowing whether they in fact operate a satisfactory pattern of work. Regular visits to teleworkers, at
times agreed with them in advance, could be made using a
check-list to ensure safety of home equipment, and also to
ask about the employee's health.

New technology agreements

If employers have negotiated such an agreement with the
trade unions representing workers, the provisions apply
equally to remote staff. Sometimes those agreements
include provision for eye tests, and not to employ people
on display equipment work who suffer from migraine or
epilepsy.

An example of health and safety guidelines

As part of their guidance for teleworkers, Lombard North
Central provide staff with a booklet on the use of display
equipment, and a check-list of general health and safety
guidelines. The staff must be aware that they are responsible for maintaining safe working practices, and for not
putting others at risk. They stipulate that they should not
move equipment without consultation with their employer. The Health and Safety Executive do not have particular guidelines for home-workers so they offer the
following points:

● the desk or table is stable and able to support the weight
of equipment,

- items on shelves are within easy reach and drawers not left open,
- the number of plug points is adequate, avoiding running several appliances from the same socket,
- lighting is adequate so that printed or screen material can be easily read,
- cables are safely routed to the work area, and carpets are smooth or taped down if necessary,
- the room is adequately ventilated (for office work, a window is sufficient),
- care is taken in positioning electric heaters in relation to office furniture,
- adequate floor-loading especially in older houses (the Health and Safety Executive consider that only if three or more four drawer cabinets are lined up will this become an issue),
- smokers should dispose of cigarettes with care.

15

Tax insurance and planning implications of working at home

This chapter outlines the main issues surrounding home-based teleworking. It is vitally important that:

- all of these issues are sorted out *before* homeworking is embarked upon,
- employers and teleworkers keep up-to-date with changes in relevant legislation,
- advice from the relevant authority in each case is always sought.

Capital Gains Tax

For the vast majority of home-based workers who use part of a room in their domestic premises, Capital Gains Tax liability should not arise. If a room in a house is used *solely* for work purposes, that part of the house may be liable pro rata for Capital Gains Tax, when the house is sold. However, if it can be demonstrated to the Inland Revenue that the part of the house used for business purposes is also occasionally used for domestic purposes, the homeworker may not be liable. If a teleworker makes claims for business expenses relating to domestic premises, this may affect a teleworker's Capital Gains Tax position. Professional advice should be sought on this point, from the Inland Revenue or an accountant.

Planning permission

In all cases, teleworkers should in theory apply to their Local Planning Authority for permission to change the use of part of a property from domestic to 'business' use but, in the vast majority of cases, teleworkers are unlikely to be refused permission. Most Councils are eager to promote employment (many self-employed people start up at home) and if home-based teleworkers' operations do not involve alterations to the domestic premises, and do not constitute a nuisance or hazard to neighbours (including increased parking) there should be no problem. The Department of Environment Circular (2/86), Development by Small Business, states clearly that the use of a room as an office would *not* normally require permission.

However, if the home operation entails a radical change from domestic use, with structural alterations to the premises, or if it impinges on the lives of others living nearby, it may become necessary to apply for a change of use, or to seek separate premises.

Teleworkers, whether home-owners or tenants must check that homeworking does not have unfortunate consequences for their homes. Generally they must:

- check that mortgage agreements are not affected by work-at-home, if they are buying their own home. Also if there are any restrictions in the house deeds, covenants and so on,
- seek permission from their landlords about working at home if they rent privately,
- check that homeworking does not affect their Council tenancy if they rent from the local council.

Uniform Business Rate (UBR)

The liability for business rating depends upon the impact and scale of the home-based work, and how much it affects the residential nature of the home and its surroundings. Thus, the vast majority of teleworkers should *not* be affected. The government's attitude to those working from home seems to be that 'where the use of domestic property for a non-domestic purpose does not materially detract from the domestic use, that should not result in that property being rated' (Lord Caithness speaking in the House of Lords, 1990). Information on the business rate should be sought from the Inland Revenue.

In Northern Ireland the rating system still applies, with similar implications to the UBR. The Local Authority in this case should be contacted for guidance.

Insurance

The insurance position varies with the employment status of the teleworker. Self-employed teleworkers should make their own insurance arrangements to cover their own safety, liability for third parties and possible additional cover for expensive electronic equipment which would not normally be covered by domestic contents insurance.

For those who are employed, where the equipment is generally owned by the employer, insurance is usually provided by the employer, with the proviso that the user does not invalidate it by moving or damaging it unnecessarily. Cover is also usually provided in respect of employee and public liability for home-based employees, by employers' insurance, but employers should consult their insurers to check if this is applicable.

Lombard North Central require teleworkers to ensure that their insurance policies are not adversely affected by working at home, and that third party personal liability cover is in force. The company offer to meet the increased cost if additional cover is needed.

16

Trade union attitudes to telework

Trade unions, both here and in the rest of Europe, have been particularly concerned about the home-based type of telework, because it has potentially the most radical effects upon the working lives of their members. Fears that it could come to resemble 'traditional' home-work or out-work used in the manufacturing sector are never far from the surface. Traditional outwork is characterized by sub-contractor status, low wages, no fringe benefits, irregular work and poor working conditions, as well as isolation from other workers, resulting in problems of trade union recruitment and organization. Added to this is the fact that some teleworkers are part-time and many in the future may be female. Trade unions have tended in the past to regard 'flexibility' as a trend which undermines their influence, and women workers are often seen as a reserve army of labour which acts as a source of 'dilution' to the full-time workforce.

As a result of these interwoven factors, many trade unions are dubious about telework, with the fiercest opposition coming from German unions (and the women's movement there) who have called for a total ban on home-based telework.

Attempts at legislation for homeworkers

In the UK, in early 1979, an attempt was made to introduce a Home-worker's Protection Bill, which would have extended basic employment rights to homeworkers, and introduced a registration scheme, but this never reached the second reading stage. During the 1980s the climate radically changed, with the Thatcher government pressing for further deregulation of the workforce: no legislation specific to homeworkers was passed, and no legal protection was extended to them. The UK trade unions have tended to vary in the evolution of their attitudes towards 'high-tech' homework, some unions remaining very opposed to it in any form, and others more willing to negotiate to try to secure reasonable terms and conditions for teleworking employees.

The TUC's attitude

In 1988 the Confederation of British Industry (CBI) and British Telecom held a conference on telework, which was addressed by the Trades Union Congress (TUC) General Secretary, Norman Willis. He did not express reservations about telework for the well-qualified professional, or managerial specialist, but was more concerned about the second wave of 'high-tech' remote workers, who will mainly be women in 'back-office' jobs, with a much weaker bargaining position. Thus, again, it is the less well-qualified who continue to be the focus of trade union anxiety. The TUC wanted its affiliated unions to participate in any decisions about the introduction of teleworking but could see its possible value in job creation both in urban and rural areas.

Attitudes of UK trade unions

With the growing interest from employers in telework in recent years, it is clear that the issue is not going to be laid to rest. Two distinct approaches are emerging among UK trade unions; one tending towards outright opposition to telework because of the view that employers are treating it as the latest form of outwork by exploiting the workforce; the other a somewhat more positive approach, accepting that the unions must come to terms with a more 'flexible' workforce, and seek to represent it, or face continued decline.

The first approach has been adopted by the Banking, Insurance and Finance Union (BIFU) who, in their paper on Homeworking, describe a number of cases where remote workers have been bullied into accepting terms and conditions less favourable than their conventional counterparts, leading to a divided and weakened workforce. The union feels that it would have much greater difficulty in recruiting homeworkers and, even if they did join, they would be less likely to participate in union activities. Thus the consequences for BIFU of a large-scale move to homeworking are potentially very damaging, and the union is determined to resist the trend.

An example of the second approach comes from the Manufacturing, Science and Finance Union (MSF), who accept that there will continue to be pressure from employers towards teleworking. The union feels that the technology can be used to enhance or degrade jobs, and the MSF's role is to try to ensure that employers use the opportunities responsibly. At the same time they are pressing the European Commission to adopt policies on homeworking as part of the Social Charter, in order to ensure at least basic employment rights to homeworkers.

Employer's homeworking guidelines

A number of employers, including BT, are working on guidelines for the use of manager's of teleworkers or homeworkers. The latest to be published is for the Civil Service. The Council of Civil Service Unions have refused to sign a circular because a number of their concerns about terms and conditions for homeworkers have not been met. The main concern is pay: homeworkers will not necessarily be given the same rates as their on-site equivalents, and departments are not obliged to give increments or to extend performance-related pay to homeworkers. A second area of contention is childcare. The unions consider that working at home is no substitute for adequate childcare arrangements, and homework is not seen as the best way of dealing with member's problems of combining paid work and family responsibilities.

The trends to date tend to confirm Mike Brocklehurst's view (1989) that a 'two-nations' approach is emerging around telework, mirroring the situation of much conventional work. Groups with scarce skills and a strong market situation – the 'elite' of the remote workforce – may, through telework, gain for themselves an extra dimension of flexibility, autonomy and freedom, whilst retaining an important foothold on the corporate career ladder, by keeping some on-site visibility. By contrast, groups whose skills are not in short supply, who are easily replaced, and have a relatively weak market situation, may often be closely monitored by the equipment, and at the same time lack the social interaction that ameliorates the monotony of the equivalent on-site job. It is unfortunate that some employers may be creating new groups of disadvantaged 'high-tech' outworkers, which could discredit home-based telework as an acceptable working pattern.

The homeworker's charter

Ursula Huws in, *The New Homeworkers* (1984), put forward a code of good practice for employers of homeworkers, which would apply equally to teleworkers:

- homeworkers working primarily for one employer or dependent on that employer for most of their work, should have employee status and be eligible for sickness, holiday, maternity, pension and training benefits pro-rata with on-site employees, due notice of redundancy and changes in employment conditions. They should have the same protection as those on-site from unfair dismissal, and the right to take part in trade union activity.

- homeworkers should be paid the same rates (pro rata for part-timers) as on-site workers doing the same or similar work. They should receive payment for overtime and unsocial hours, (where they are caused by work pressure from employers). They should also be eligible for extra payments, such as profit sharing to which on-site workers are entitled.
- all expenses incurred in the course of their work should be reimbursed by the employer.
- social isolation should be minimized by face-to-face meetings or periodic social get-togethers. When workers use electronic communications systems, they should be able to communicate with each other, as well as with the employer.
- homeworkers should be kept informed of organizational developments and consulted about changes which could affect them. They should be eligible for training or retraining in order to adapt to these changes.
- whenever possible, homeworkers should be eligible for promotion.
- those wishing to take up on-site work should be allowed to do so.
- all internal vacancies should be notified to homeworkers and they should be encouraged to apply for them.
- periods of homework should count equally with on-site employment towards pensions, sick pay or maternity provisions, or any other benefit related to seniority.
- teleworkers should be provided by the employer with equipment, fitments and furnishings necessary for the home work-station. These should be safe, and be checked and maintained regularly to a high standard.

17

Telework and environmental issues

Because telework can involve the extensive relocation of work, and the 'reshaping' of organizations, it has been linked with various environmental issues, in particular transportation patterns and pollution. In this chapter the possible environmental impact of telework is discussed under the headings:

- transportation policy and energy use,
- trends in the geography of work,
- the telecommunications infrastructure.

Transportation policy and energy use

One of the trigger factors leading employers to consider telework as well as wholesale relocation, is worsening traffic congestion and associated air pollution, particularly in large cities, as well as a poor public transport system. These problems are causing difficulties for employers in attracting and retaining employees, and leading them to question why they remain in an increasingly unattractive and expensive environment.

The Policy Studies Institute (PSI) in, *Britain in 2010* (1991), predicts that we are going to see further measures to check the rise of private cars in cities, beyond the compulsory fitting of catalytic converters to new cars from 1993. These could include eliminating tax breaks on company cars, tax incentives for 'cleaner cars' – diesel for example – or smaller, fuel-efficient cars, and charges for the use of certain roads (toll roads).

The environmental pressure group Friends of the Earth in their book, *Reviving the City* (1991), feel that a radical policy shift by government is necessary to persuade them to develop public transport and encourage cycle usage as well as curbing road building and out-of-town shopping centres which lead to increased car usage.

However, these are all long-term aims: in the short-term, telework could provide one possible solution to transport problems for individuals. It is unlikely to be taken up on such a scale that it totally transforms patterns of traffic movement, or significantly reduces traffic volume. Jack Nilles, in the book *The Information Technology Revolution* (1982), estimated in the early 1970s that if one-seventh of urban commuting were replaced by telework, the USA would no longer need to import oil, and air pollution would decrease accordingly. We feel that the future extent of telework in the UK in the short term would not be so great as to make such a significant impact.

Nevertheless, the pollution control measures which will be needed if the UK is to keep carbon dioxide emissions down to 1990 levels, which is the current target, might have a bearing on the long-term decisions of employers. The PSI feels that the costs of car transport in particular may rise to such an extent that employers may reconsider seriously the work patterns of their employees. Company cars will cease to be a 'perk', perhaps replaced in some cases by a 'flexi-place' policy for employees.

Another consideration is the amount of energy used by teleworkers operating at home, compared to the conventional commuting office worker. Some teleworkers would be field employees who would continue to use cars or public transport, so their energy savings would be negligible. Those who combine office and homework, or who are entirely home-based, would use less energy in commuting, but there are also other considerations. Huws, Korte and Robinson (1990) point out that heating and lighting the remote workstation may represent a relatively inefficient use of energy. Heating a large space for the benefit of one individual, instead of many workers sharing an office, may be wasteful. Also, if telework resulted in a shift of the workforce to rural areas, there might be fewer journeys, but these would be longer, and because of our extremely poor rural public transport, the overall result might be an actual increase in car usage, for shopping and leisure use.

Trends in the geography of work

The main trend in the movement of jobs since the 1970s has been for private sector service jobs to move from London to the South East and adjoining Regions. This has benefited old industrial towns around London (for example Luton, Reading and Slough) and major provincial cities further afield (for example, Bristol, Ipswich and Cambridge). In parallel with this movement, there has been a 'suburbanization' of office work in metropolitan areas. In the United States, Margrethe Olson (1981) found a similar trend, with some companies using telework as an alternative to conventional on-site office work. Barbara Baran (1988), in a study of the US insurance sector, found that offices were moving to smaller towns to access the suburban, white, female, well-educated workforce also with a 'trend' towards employers using telework.

This movement out of the city centre has followed a much longer period of loss of blue-collar employment from the inner city areas of the large conurbations. This has been due to the decline in manufacturing employment. If these trends continue, the inner-city would become bereft of both white and blue-collar jobs, and commentators predict either that they would become pleasant spaces with recreational facilities, or on the other hand, areas of extreme deprivation cut off from wealthier suburban centres.

The PSI predicts that the drift of offices to more pleasant suburban locations or nearby small towns will continue, but firms may choose to retain a 'strategic core' of functions in city centres. There may also continue to be some movement into the cities of offices, for prestige or operational reasons, despite continuing high costs and inconvenience, so that commercial centres will survive into the next century.

Telework has also been suggested as a way of regenerating depressed regions. There is some evidence of a limited movement of self-contained, back-office functions further afield to satellites in the old manufacturing cities and towns of the North, as well as wholesale relocations of financial and mainly administrative organizations to cities for example in Wales and Northern Ireland.

The impact of telework on rural areas appears very limited so far, although there is a growing number of mainly self-employed teleworkers in remote rural areas, doing activities which are location independent. For example, the Highlands and Islands Development Board found quite a number of people in Scotland already working in this way. The 'telecottage' movement is gaining ground, but very slowly: only a handful are up and running, with another thirty centres at the planning stage. What impact on rural labour markets telework will have is not yet clear.

If it were to grow significantly, the fear among some rural pressure groups, such as the Campaign for the Preservation of Rural England (CPRE), is that telework would suck in the relatively well-off incomers from urban centres who would further push up prices of sought-after rural property, but it would not actually enable disadvantaged local people to enjoy better quality jobs.

The telecommunications infrastructure

The UK is currently developing a digital network, which brings a closer convergence between computers and telecommunications as both use the same binary code language. Digital networks are faster and more reliable than electro-mechanical systems, and offer better facilities for the transmission of computer data, text, pictures and fax as well as voice communications. The UK will have about 3000 digital exchanges by 1992, linking large and medium-sized towns. More significant even than the development of a digital exchange network is the issue of creating a 'national grid' of optical fibre cables linking up all homes. A fibre optic, or broadband network could give an almost unlimited capacity for carrying TV channels, high-quality audio-visuals, and interactive links to facilitate video-conferencing, telebanking and shopping as well as teleworking.

However, such a development is very costly, and cable companies are only likely to provide them where there is the likelihood of a return on investment from the television element. British Telecom, however, is still precluded from carrying television down its optical fibre telephone cables and, without potential profits from television, is probably unlikely to further invest on a large scale in such a national grid. Thus the provision of optical fibre cable is likely to remain patchy, restricted to areas where it is commercially attractive.

The current costing of telephone usage by distance may also inhibit the development of telework in some cases. If tariffs were based on volume rather than distance, this would remove a cost-barrier. Huws, Korte and Robinson (1990) found that some telework schemes, with high 'on-line' usage, were only viable within a local call-charge area, which could mean that the decentralization of 'back-office' functions such as data entry or word-processing with data links to a central office may be fairly short-range geographically.

The telecommunications infrastructure could also inhibit the revitalization of rural labour markets. A Rural Development Commission Report in 1989, *Telecommunications in Rural England*, found that many services are concentrated in areas of highest demand, and some services are not available in rural areas, or are charged at a higher rate away from concentrations of population. Exceptions to this general trend are Northern Ireland and the Highlands and Islands which are being converted to digital working ahead of other mainly rural areas.

The future development of telecommunications technology is, however sophisticated, only an enabling factor, and will not of itself, ensure the spread of teleworking. Socio-economic and psychological factors are much more important when an attempt is made to assess to what extent telework will be adopted as a work pattern. Information technology will provide the potential for changing the shape and nature of work organizations, but as yet this potential remains largely untapped.

18

Telework and the European Community

The completion of the single market of the European Community (EC) in 1992 is forecast to lead to more intense trading competition, as well as opportunities in a much larger potential market for goods and services, without artificial tariff barriers. However, because the UK is on the outside edge of Europe, and the Channel Tunnel development has not yet been followed by any definite plans for high-speed rail links even as far as London, there are fears being expressed that only parts of the UK will benefit in trade terms from 1992.

Regional imbalances in the UK

It may well be that the 'Golden Triangle', which is the part of England roughly south of a line from the Wash to the Bristol Channel, will be the only part of the UK that will benefit from the single market in terms of employment. This area is already much more favourably placed than other parts of the UK. It has been the focus of recent service sector employment growth, and has the highest economic activity rates for both sexes. It contains two important clusters of firms developing information technology products, along the M4 corridor, and in the Cambridge area.

Thus the 'Golden Triangle', despite setbacks in recessionary periods, tends to exhibit all the problems of a buoyant labour market: high overhead and housing costs, skills shortages (even in economic downturns), environmental problems of traffic congestion and pressure on under-funded public transport provision. These problems may lead more employers to consider telework, in all its various forms, as one solution to the overheating of this part of the country.

Whether the increasing Europeanization of the UK, which is predicted by the Policy Studies Institute (PSI), will lead to an increase in telework *between* European countries is still an open question: certainly the long-term aim of EC member countries is a convergence of the telecommunications system which would facilitate this. An increased mobility of labour between countries is forecast, but initially mainly among the more privileged groups such as professionals and technical specialists. Telework holds out the possibility of undertaking information-based work in whichever location is preferred, so that future teleworkers could live in France or much further afield, linked electronically to employers in the UK (or vice versa, of course).

EC regional policy

There is a great deal of interest in using computer and telecommunications technology to redress the considerable regional imbalances in the EC, particularly the relative deprivation in the rural areas of Europe. A group of advisers to the European Commission reported in 1989 on how this imbalance could be redressed. By providing an up-to-date telecommunications infrastructure, the rural areas could be given an opportunity to compete on an equal basis with urban areas. To this end they advocated research into many possible ways of supporting small businesses in rural areas by opening up access to business services and larger markets, improving local commercial and social services, and reversing the trend to out-migration of young people, and encouraging in-migration of working people by developing teleworking.

One of the schemes which has been supported by the Community is the Highlands and Islands development of digital exchanges and Integrated Services Digital Networks. This area of Scotland is the least populated area within the European Community.

The Social Charter

The completion of the single market in 1992, as well as opening up opportunities for trade, could also have some negative aspects for the workforce. Despite EC forecasts of long-term employment growth, there could well be some initial contraction in the jobs market. There is also the possibility of 'social dumping', whereby jobs are moved away from richer member states to poorer countries or regions where labour costs are much lower, and there is less employment protection. This fear is leading to pressure for a further equalization of social rights, in the form of the Social Charter. This may affect teleworkers because it will include rights for part-timers, as well as policies on childcare, where the UK tends to lag far behind other European member countries. There may also be pressure from trade unions to go further, and give some employment protection to homeworkers, although this is not on the agenda at present.

There is still a great deal of work to be done before the legal framework exists to enforce Social Charter provisions: some European governments and employers' groupings will continue to resist its implementation because they believe it will impede the operation of market forces within the EC. The UK Conservative governments have consistently opposed the Charter because it is seen to jeopardize a deregulatory approach to the labour market — a key element of their employment policy.

19

The future of telework

During the last few years there has been a much greater interest from employers in 'atypical' patterns of work, and a greater willingness to experiment with these when organizations are faced with human resource problems. These problems may stem from tight labour markets in periods of economic expansion, or from fluctuating demand and cost-cutting during periods of recession. Telework, as one alternative working pattern, can address these problems. Between industries and sectors, and over time, the problems may ebb and flow, but telework, which offers time and locational flexibility, will continue to offer one solution.

Growth patterns

There seem to be two ways in which corporate telework is growing within work organizations:

- in an ad hoc or 'organic' way, where it is used in individualistic ways to solve one-off human resource problems. There are few or no formal rules or procedures.
- bureaucratically, or in a 'top-down' way, where telework is introduced in a planned way with formal rules and procedures. Sometimes, it involves whole job categories moving to telework.

Sometimes the organic approach eventually leads to the more bureaucratic approach, and the emergence of codes of practice in organizations often comes as a result of a head office becoming aware of a number of local initiatives, and rationalizing employment practices to achieve some common standards for all employees. Both approaches are equally valid, given a responsible and humane approach by employers and individual managers.

Attitudes to telework

Empirica carried out large-scale attitude surveys in the mid-1980s, which are detailed in Huws, Korte and Robinson's book. One survey was of business leaders in Germany, France, Italy and the UK. The results showed that at the time telework was a very minor interest for European managers. They were generally conservative and unwilling to change. The main reasons for rejecting telework were:

- perceived difficulties of organizing it,
- a lack of need for change,
- inadequate and costly telecommunications.

The survey demonstrates clearly that there must be very strong reasons for managers to opt for telework, which is very much in line with Olson's (1981) findings from the USA. The sectors showing most interest were banking and insurance, the retail sector in some countries, small business and the self-employed (in the latter case often as a way of sub-contracting office work).

Potential teleworkers, again from the same four countries, were also asked about their interest – in this case about homebased telework. There was least interest in Germany (8.5 per cent), but most interest in the UK (23 per cent). The greatest interest was shown by those familiar with the equipment, and already using computers as part of their job. Single and childless households tended to wish to retain links with a workplace, whereas people with children were more amenable to the idea of home-based work. There was no significant difference between men's and women's attitudes to telework, but women with children were slightly more interested particularly where they were second-earners. Therefore, people's family and household circumstances were important in influencing their attitudes, but what it demonstrates most clearly is that employees must have very strong reasons to consider telework as an option. It also shows that the workplace is still an important source of friendship and social contact, particularly among single people. The Henley Centre for Forecasting survey (1988) also found that, for all occupational groupings, work outside the home remains the greatest source of friendship, and twice as many of their employed sample would consider working at home part of the time than were prepared to work at home *all* the time (50 per cent compared to 25 per cent).

Human resource issues

Some of the problems surrounding telework which we have discussed in this book are unlikely to be completely resolved, though we feel that it is important to try to do so. Teleworkers and their employers will continue to live with the problems in order to reap the benefits. These include social isolation, lack of career progression and supervision problems.

Although telework has been marketed predominantly to 'elite' groups within the workforce, where it can bestow a number of advantages in increased autonomy, independence and job satisfaction, with few of the disadvantages, it is clear that this may not be the case among other groups. There is now a growth in the use of homebased telework for back-office functions, where the outcome could be very different, if employers use it only as a cost-cutting tactic. The second wave of teleworkers is also more likely to be female, with childcare responsibilities, so that the question arises as to whether responsible employers should use telework, or use other ways of enabling women to work on-site; in other words, is telework compatible with the aim of equal opportunities?

Technological developments

Telework is a phenomenon which will not disappear, and can be one of a number of developments which are changing the structure of organizations. Modern office technology, personal computers, VDUs and electronic mail, are often used in a way which leads to a reduction in the amount of face-to-face interaction *within* the workplace: remote work takes this one stage further. It is probably still true that 'face-to-face relationships can be thought of as the glue that holds organizations together' (Edgar Schein), but many alternative, or additional modes of communication, are now available. Often people need to learn the best and most appropriate ways of using these, but research suggests that only systems which fulfil a particular need will develop. Also there is often a long time lag between the availability of the technology and its 'take-off' in the market – a good example is the facsimile machine which has been around for a long time, but has only recently become a necessity for organizations and individuals.

We think that telework, along with other alternative work patterns, will probably continue to grow slowly and patchily, mainly in response to employers' human resource problems. We do not predict that it will become the norm, not only because of the many jobs which cannot be undertaken in this way, but also because of the persistence of important social and psychological barriers within work organizations.

20

Two telework case studies

Digital Equipment Company

Digital is an American company which trades worldwide. As well as being the world's largest manufacturer of mini-computers it is also unique in that it is a world leader in networking computers. The corporate culture at Digital is very entrepreneurial, and the senior management encourages innovation in all functions. At Digital, we spoke to Philip Scott, Human Relations Consultant, Jo Brayshaw, UK Selling Training Manager, and Mike Hinds, Organizational Development Consultant.

Mike Hinds explained that it was his idea when he was Selling Training Manager to move towards more flexible working patterns. Much sales training work is done in remote offices and in hotels, so it appeared a logical step to develop a teleworking pilot in this area of work. Jo Brayshaw's previous post was as manager of sales trainers, with particular responsibility for the people and career development aspects. Another reason for choosing this area for remote work was that previously salesmen were seconded into sales training for two-year periods, which meant relocation from all parts of the UK to South-East England. The company was facing ever-increasing relocation costs for this group, with the additional problem of moving them back to their original base a couple of years later.

The scheme began with nine people, some of whom have now gone back into the field. At present there are five people who are either home-based or based in a remote office. Another teleworker has negotiated a contract whereby he works independently half the time and for Digital the other half.

Jo Brayshaw is in a unique position because she has herself experienced life as a teleworker in the group of which she is now manager. She began teleworking whilst on maternity leave with her second child, and worked remotely for a period of almost four years, during which time she also moved much further away from the Reading office. She is still home-based, but spends some time in the office when necessary. Without the ability to be home-based and to work in a flexible way, she would not have been able to develop her career, and is therefore highly committed to the scheme.

Philip Scott's involvement has been at a more strategic level, on a programme called 'People for the Nineties', which involves researching developments in the field of flexible working practices and helping the company develop a variety of such practices in order to meet both operational and human needs. He worked closely with Mike and Jo when they were developing the Sales Training remote working scheme. There are a number of different projects being developed by Digital in the UK involving various forms of flexibility, not just telework.

Our three interviewees were essentially in agreement in their comments and views on teleworking, which were as follows:

Telework offers the advantage of allowing people to work wherever necessary, not just in the office or at home but also whilst travelling or in clients' premises – in fact almost anywhere. Mobile 'phones and laptop computers are extending the range still further, the latter now facilitating two-way information links rather than just the ability to download data at the end of a day's work.

An organization needs a culture which supports the sort of innovation which we are developing and Digital has always had a commitment to developing systems using our own technology. The whole company could not exist now without its electronic mail system, and the technology is now second-nature to us.

The cost of relocating people was climbing steeply, and

we were ending up with some really huge bills. There was the problem of secondees going back to their home-base after secondment. Office space here in Reading was also at a premium. Pressure to save office space and to utilize what we had in a different way was acute. What we have done is to have some dedicated space for the administrative staff based here in Reading, and in addition non-dedicated workstations for people coming into the office at various times, plus some informal meeting space, which is shared by the team. For most of the time the trainers are out in the field, working, and this is a much better use of the available facilities.

We did not at any time make the move out of the office compulsory, and if people feel that it is not working out for them they can return to an office base. We want people to feel comfortable with the scheme, and with the fact that they are being experimented upon. The scheme has been in operation for two years now. We use telework very flexibly, in order to suit both company and individual needs, so there is no time limit on how long someone will telework. There is a very wide spectrum of people here with varying needs and aspirations. Some will probably never want to work in an office again; others will.

There is also a lot of freedom for people to organize their own time, within a broad framework of rules. A working party was set up to work out what the rules should be, with the full participation of potential teleworkers and those who would be working back at base as support. Both groups had a chance at an early stage to work through the advantages and disadvantages of the project.

One thing we were firm about was the amount of state-of-the-art kit we would allow staff to have. In this way we tried to keep costs down in case the pilot didn't work out. Also we had clear rules about contact 'phone numbers, and decided it was not acceptable for this group to rely on answerphones, which really are dead-ends for clients. Calls are always redirected to the central office if people are not available.

Another issue which is crucial is establishing the necessary high level of trust between teleworker and manager — in fact within the group as a whole. Each team-member has a job-plan with specific goals, and they are encouraged to take responsibility for their own self-development. Many of our trainers are away for two-week periods, and also may be unavailable at other times, so it is crucial for the support group always to know what is happening – this is all part of an individual's responsibility. Otherwise it just cannot work. The support people are absolutely pivotal to this experiment and must be respected.

There is a tradition within the company of people having terminals at home, and also of us retaining the talents of people on maternity leave for example, so this particular development can be seen as a further extension of that tradition. The fact that it is labelled telework is not really important.

We also have lots of other experiments running, including term-time contracts, taking on older workers and part-time contracts, so it must be seen in the overall context of a very flexible attitude to human resource issues, in order to get the best out of people.

The staff who have been involved with the telework project have all had previous company experience, and we are now looking for some more recruits with particular qualities. What we look for are high work-standards, good motivation, plus a strong emphasis on how well people will fit in with the way we work. We feel it is crucial for teleworkers to have an understanding of the company and how it works. We don't feel it would work if we recruited them to telework from day one. We would not consider letting people work remotely if there was any doubt about their work standards as on-site employees either.

Team-building and working as a group are very important and working remotely means a greater emphasis on keeping people together – it is more difficult to keep that going. Each member of the group has a half-day monthly meeting with the manager, and they meet as a team for a day every month. Half of the day is spent on reviewing objectives and the other half on getting together and just talking to one another exchanging information – these are known as 'sacred days'. If even one person is absent on those days the group feels let down because they miss out on some information and contact. So, even with electronic mail, telephones and all the high-tech communications we have, there is still no substitute for face-to-face meetings to glue the group together.

The line-manager's role in all this demands some very particular skills too. Not many managers have these skills, which involve an ability to cope with a high degree of complexity and to plan ahead, orderliness and a very people-centred approach to management. In many ways women managers may have these skills more than men, and sadly they are often not skills which have been valued in the past in getting up the corporate ladder. A manager of teleworkers also needs someone to ensure their corporate development, because it is all too easy not to be visible and to be passed over. Digital has a system of career-development contracts between the individual and the manager. Career development is considered important at every level, and remote workers are part of that process – it makes no difference where they work.

Childcare is another aspect about which there are widespread misconceptions. It is really not acceptable to fit work around the children: proper provision is necessary, and we feel that it is the responsibility of the teleworker to organize this.

The home work-space is also considered. There must be a space for working, ideally a study or less ideally a spare bedroom, but working on the dining-room table is not acceptable. Family attitudes towards the person working at home are also borne in mind – they must be positive. There is also the fact that trainers are away from home for extended periods. Peers and friends also have adjustments to make.

The office is really not the ideal place for doing work which requires concentration, so that giving people the flexibility to work away from that environment, to write reports or prepare things which require thought, is to an organization's advantage. The office is good for meetings, for co-ordinating people's work, but is often a somewhat frenetic place.

The magic ingredient for making telework a success is having the right culture, which we think that we have. You just cannot bolt telework onto an organization where the

culture is one of low trust, because it simply will not work.
Another spin-off for us, being in the business solutions
business, is that the success of our experiments may help
people in other organizations to solve their own problems.

Company X

Company X is a buoyant high-profile nationally based
company, operating in the financial services sector of the
economy. It is a unionized company. The human resource
function in Company X is proactive and has an input into
corporate strategy, enabling policy to be made which takes
account of this resource. Advice is given to the Board and
recommendations made in the various policy areas. The
chief Industrial Relations Manager has been closely
involved in developing an operational policy on teleworking:

> Telework is seen by the Company as one of several options
> available in making best use of our people. It is seen as an
> attractive option capable of filling gaps left by such things
> as return-to-work schemes, maternity provisions and
> career breaks. Any employer who is planning over the long
> term, say over a five-year period, must have policies in
> place to attract, and continue to attract, the right sort of
> people. Although in the short term the recession has
> eclipsed concerns about the demographic cliff, we must
> not lose sight of the longer term. We must ensure that we
> remain in the market for the best staff.
>
> It is really a mistake to think short term in the human
> resource area because people need to be recruited and
> trained now ready for the boom times. A company cannot
> ensure that the necessary resources are in place simply by
> reacting suddenly to a period of economic expansion. You
> would not be able to operate at the optimum if you tried to
> do that, and it would be reflected ultimately in the bottom-
> line. Profits would suffer. That is why we try to look ahead
> a little and get it right.
>
> A key factor that we as a company considered when

adopting a telework scheme was that of the continually spiralling overhead costs involved in employing people. These seem to have no end. Also, from the employees' point of view, commuting is no longer a pleasure and the prospects for the future look worse. The statistics show that transport problems will be exacerbated – this applies both to road and rail transport. Telework offers one solution for some people, depending on how they feel about it. It also offers an opportunity to release office space and the possibility of cost reductions. Telework can offer benefits to both employer and employee. People have the opportunity for flexibility in organizing their own patterns of working, and planning their own lives.

At Company X, before introducing our telework scheme, we did a broad cost-benefit analysis. It was not terribly detailed because, to a certain extent, with the pilot scheme we were inevitably moving into unknown territory. For example, until we had actually set up home work-stations, we could not make accurate judgements about costs. We found that there were computer hardware and software items we needed to buy in for a small group of people. That's inevitably more expensive than doing it for larger groups. The teleworkers needed the same degree of access, with the same quality and response times as on-site staff.

We bought in consultancy expertise to help us set up the scheme. With hindsight I think we had the necessary knowledge in-house, and that our consultants learned as much from us as we did from them in the end. The advantage was that their presence saved us time. There were a number of jobs which the consultants identified as suitable for telework. One area where we got very positive responses was the IT area and there seemed to be a need for a package to offer staff both to attract and retain them. There were two other areas which we have also considered. We talked to the staff about the pros and cons of this form of work and gave them time to consider it. Then we went back and asked who would be prepared to commit themselves to such a change, and discussed the scheme with them in more detail. It is very important that people are volunteers and have positive commitment.

Line managers are also absolutely crucial to the success

of any such development. There is a distinctly different relationship between the manager and the teleworker compared to the manager and the on-site worker. Higher levels of trust are required and managers have to acquire new skills. Objective-setting becomes more important, and people need to think more carefully about what they are requiring their staff to do. I think many managers could supervise remote workers, but a minority may find it impossible to manage remotely – in the same way that some people will not be able to work remotely.

Once the scheme was started we had a number of on-site staff becoming quite envious of the teleworkers' ability to plan their own work-time, and reconsidering their initial decision not to participate. We haven't experienced on-site staff failing to take others' home-based work seriously. Teleworkers have a lot of leeway to decide their own schedules, within the constraints of each individual job. Ways of working are decided between the individual and the line manager.

In terms of teleworkers' productivity, we have noticed an improvement in quality more than quantity of work. One reason for this is the absence of distractions when you are working at home. For some areas of work, especially where concentration is needed, the office is probably not the best place. In some cases we have also noticed that people can work more quickly.

Teleworkers need both the right personality and attitude to work, and if the scheme takes off in the next few years we are going to have to define these attributes more closely, because we will be recruiting teleworkers from the open market. They need to combine the ability to cope with isolation and be self-starters with the somewhat paradoxical ability to operate successfully as part of a team.

We consider it very important that our teleworkers remain full members of the organization and we provide opportunities for them to meet, not just for reviewing their work, but also to gossip, exchange views and remain part of a team. For the pilot we went further and organized feed-back sessions with members of the working-party to give people an opportunity to discuss their experiences.

Another aspect of the approach that we are taking is that

there is no time limit set for people to work remotely – some will wish to do it long term, others may wish to return to office-based work. We also try to create an internal labour market; teleworkers, like other staff, are eligible for openings within the company. They are encouraged to develop themselves, which is healthy from their own as well as from the company's viewpoint.

The limits on the use of telework in an organization are set by the organization and its employees. The opportunities are there in the future for expanding remote work, encompassing some line management jobs. Some jobs may not be suitable and some people may not wish to work in unconventional ways, but beyond that you can take telework as far as you like.

Security of data is a potential problem dependent on the sensitivity of the data. There have to be strong security guidelines and controls together with an extension of the trust that exists between a company and its employees. We believe that if we take all prudent measures to protect our interests, then the degree of risk will be no greater than that normally experienced in a traditional environment.

As regards home workspace, we insist that the home has sufficient space for the work to be carried out in a safe and comfortable manner which does not interfere with domestic arrangements. We don't want work at home to be a burden, which it would be if someone was trying to fit one more activity into an already confined space.

As far as planning permission is concerned, we have had no problems so far. We insist that our teleworkers check things like leases and tenancies before they begin this form of work, and we have checked everything out with the Inland Revenue. I feel that they have been rather rigid and bureaucratic in their attitude, and overall are very negative.

We do give various allowances to our teleworkers which we will be reviewing before the scheme is adopted more generally, but the philosophy is not of cost-cutting but of fairness as between on-site and remote workers. We are not in the business of pushing our people into self-employment and avoiding redundancy payments, or of ducking the costs of directly employing people. This also extends to fringe benefits, where we are trying to ensure a common level of provision between different types of workers. We are also looking at whether we need to continue to pay Location Allowances to remote staff and the present indications are that we will.

Health and safety legislation presents a number of difficulties. It is our intention to apply the same standards that we require in any office location, which means full compliance extending beyond legislative requirements to the adoption of good practice as a matter of policy. This is controlled within a traditional office environment by regular checks to ensure adherence to standards – such checks are not as easily achieved in a home-based office. Individual teleworkers will have to adopt a greater degree of responsibility for the environment that they work in, although we will supply guidelines, support and training if required.

The attitude of the unions to this issue is interesting. We recognize two unions: one readily accepts the principle of teleworking and seems quite positive in support of the introduction of the opportunity to work in this way. The other is opposed as a matter of policy, which constrains their negotiators, who publicly protest but privately realize that they can't stand in the way of progress. We believe that the opposition from one union reflects that union's insecurity about the prospects of trying to control, organize and represent a scattered workforce. It will, if sufficient numbers are involved, give them a number of problems that they will have to overcome. Their solution at the moment seems to be Luddite: oppose and use scare tactics to unsettle people who are considering this option, for example suggesting that this is another attempt at the creation of an isolated and exploitable workforce – absolute rubbish that reflects their weakness rather than reality.

If we found ourselves in a situation where they opposed the scheme absolutely and refused sensible negotiations, then we would have to impose the option. We really couldn't accept a situation where their insecurity affected our commercial vision to that degree. Interestingly, as far as teleworking is concerned, it seems that this is an issue where at least one of our unions is talking a different language to their members and seems to be a long way behind them in their thinking. Unions are going to have to wake up to the fact that their members want to telework.

I think that the concept of telework will grow not only because of the environmental pressures that we discussed earlier, but also because people's attitudes have changed and they are now more willing to take charge of their own work-lives. People may wish to see more of their families and fit work around these priorities, and flexible modes of work offer greater possibilities of doing that as well.

Telework will grow as telecommunications improve, but it is difficult to measure its full potential. It depends on so many factors outside of an employer's control, but all of the original ingredients – costs, transport, quality of life, available technology – seem set to make this option more and more attractive to both companies and individuals. I believe that the core of the business will continue in the foreseeable future to be office-based, with growing support by networked teleworkers, perhaps comprising up to 30 per cent of the workforce early next century. The activity will probably centre initially in the South, recognizing the immediate problems and benefits there, but eventually I believe it will be commonplace to see all the major players offering teleworking anywhere in the country as one of a portfolio of employment choices designed to attract and retain the best quality staff.

References and guide to further reading

Bailyn, L. (1988) 'Freeing work from the constraints of location and time' in *New Technology, Work and Employment*, Vol. 3, No. 2, Autumn.

Banking Insurance and Finance Union (1990) *Homeworking*, BIFU.

Baran, B. (1988) 'Office automation and women's work' in Pahl, R. E. (ed.) *On Work*, Blackwell.

Brandt, S. (1983) 'Working at home' in *Office Technology and People*, Elsevier Science Publishers.

Brocklehurst, M. (1989) 'Homeworking and the new technology: the reality and the rhetoric', *Personnel Review*, Vol. 18, No. 2, MCB University Press.

Curson C. (ed.) (1986) *Flexible Patterns of Work*, Institute of Personnel Management.

European Commisison (1989) *Opportunities for Applications of Information and Communication Technologies in Rural Areas*, European Commission, Brussels.

Forester, T. (ed.) (1989) *Computers in the Human Context*, Blackwell.

Friends of the Earth (1991) *Reviving the City: Towards Sustainable Urban Development*, Friends of the Earth.

Guardian (1991) 'VDUs OK' Computer Guardian, 21 March.

Hakim, C. (1987) *Homebased Work in Britain*, Research Paper No. 60, Department of Employment.

Handy, C. (1985) *The Future of Work*, Blackwell.

Handy, C. (1989) *The Age of Unreason*, Business Books.

Health and Safety Executive (1990) *Working with VDUs*, Health and Safety Executive.

Henley Centre for Forecasting (1988) *A Cost/Benefit Analysis of Teleworking*, Henley Centre for Forecasting.

Huws, U. (1984) *The New Homeworkers*, Low Pay Unit.

Huws, U., Korte, W., and Robinson, S. (1990) *Telework: Towards the Elusive Office*, Wiley.

Industrial Relations Review and Report (1988) 'Teleworking-flexibility with remote control', No. 430, 13 December.

Industrial Relations Review and Report (1991) 'Civil Service issues homeworking guidelines', No. 481, 8 February.

International Labour Office (1990) *Conditions of Work Digest: Telework*, Vol. 9, No. 1, ILO, Geneva.

IT World (1991) 'On Teleworking and Future Patterns of Employment', Industrial Society Conference on *Teleworking in Local Authorities*, 29 January.

Judkins, P., West, D., and Drew, J. (1985) *Networking in Organisations – The Rank Xerox Experiment*, Gower.

Kinsman, F. (1987) *The Telecommuters*, Wiley.

Leighton, P. and Syrett, M. (1989) *New Work Patterns – Putting Policy into Practice*, Pitman.

National Economic Development Office (1989) *Defusing the Demographic Time Bomb*, NEDO/TA.

Nilles, J. (1982) 'Teleworking from home' in *The Information Technology Revolution*, Forester T. (ed.), Blackwell.

Olson, M. (1981) in *Office Work in the Home: Scenarios and Prospects for the 1990s*, Diebold Group, New York.

Peters, T. and Waterman, R. (1982) *In Search of Excellence: Lessons from America's Best Run Companies*, Harper and Row.

Policy Studies Institute (1991) *Britain in 2010*, P.S.I. Publishing.

Rees, D. (1991) *The Skills of Management*, 3rd edn., Routledge.

Robertson, J. (1985) *Future Work*, Gower.

Rothwell, S. (1987) 'How to manage from a distance', *Personnel Management*, September.

Rural Development Commission (1989) *Telecommunications in Rural England*, Rural Development Commission Report No. 2.

Taylor, F. W. (1911) *Scientific Management*, Harper and Bros.

Toffler, A. (1981) *The Third Wave*, Pan Books.

Training Standards Advisory Service (1989) *Evaluation of Remote Working*, Training Agency.